A BREATH OF BORDER AIR

LAVINIA DERWENT

A Breath of Border Air

Illustrated by Elizabeth Haines

ARROW BOOKS

Arrow Books Limited
17–21 Conway Street, London W I P 6JD

An imprint of the Hutchinson Publishing Group

London Melbourne Sydney Auckland
Johannesburg and agencies
throughout the world

First published by Hutchinson 1975
Arrow edition 1977
Reprinted 1977 (twice), 1979 and 1982

Set in Monotype Bembo

Made and printed in Great Britain
by The Anchor Press Ltd
Tiptree, Essex

ISBN 0 09 914020 9

To Jessie

Contents

1. Gaol in the Garret

I was thoughtless enough to be born in a snowstorm. February-fill-the-dyke. Think of the trouble it caused the doctor who had to plough seven long miles through snowdrifts just for the purpose of bringing me into the world.

'An' him wi' better things to do,' Jessie often told me. 'Fashious bairn! Ye micht hae waited.'

I had to wait long enough for my first outing. Six weeks or more, and then I was carried high above the hedgerows in a world that was still snow-white. The drifts lay long on that windswept hillside. The farmhouse, the cottages, and the fields seemed locked for ever in the icy grip of winter; and I used to wonder in later years if I would ever see the black earth again or the ripe corn standing in stooks in the fields.

Yet, looking back, it is the long sunny days of summer that I remember best, stretching into eternity, like the for-ever-and-ever in the Bible, when I ran barefoot all over the farm and never thought of yesterday or tomorrow.

The immediate moment was mine, to be filled to overflowing with activities far more engrossing than any of later years, profitless pursuits though they were. I found endless enjoyment in playing long lone games with a burst rubber ball, spying on a bird building its nest, hunting for pheasants' feathers, tumbling head-over-heels down a haystack, swinging backwards and forwards on a creaking gate, listening to the cry of the whaup, watching the shepherd rounding up the sheep. Always watching and listening.

'Man-lassie, what are ye glowerin' at?'

Jock-the-herd always addressed me as Man-lassie till I began to wonder if it was maybe my name.

'I'm just watching.'

There was so much to watch, even the changing expression on a calf's face when it licked my fingers, or on a human being's, though there were few enough of them around. The only crowd I ever saw was a flock of sheep, and the word passer-by had no meaning for me.

The farm was hidden away from the main road, with no signpost to say where the steep track led to, lost amongst trees and hills as if it had been dumped down and forgotten. The farmhouse itself was like a child's drawing, stark and bare, with walls three feet thick, which had withstood hundreds of years of rough wind and weather. The Big Hoose, the cottagers called it.

The outhouses nearby – the cart-shed, the barns, the stables, the byre, the bields for sheep and cattle – were happy hunting-grounds for a young explorer. Frightening, too, with cocks and hens flying out from dark corners, great workhorses stamping their giant feet, pigs grunting and squealing, the bull bellowing and pawing the ground, rats rustling under the straw. The ceaseless sounds were as unconnected as an orchestra tuning up. And as exciting.

There seemed no end to the restless activity of animal-life. Tails whisked, heads tossed, feet stamped, beaks pecked.

Turkeys fluffed out their feathers, roosters spread their wings, and the sheep munched from morning till night. I used to wonder if they were chewing gum and if their jaws never grew tired. Only the scarecrows stood still and quiet in the fields. The tattie-bogles, Jessie called them.

The fields themselves were full of surprises, changing their names depending on the rotation of crops. The corn-field would suddenly become the turnip-field, or the tattie-field change its identity when sown with barley. But others had more permanent names. The three-cornered field was called the Cockit Hat; there was the Lang Field, the Heathery-Hill, and the Cow-gang where the cows used to go and chew up everything they could find. Buttercups, daisies, clover, marsh-marigolds, primroses – everything was grist to their gullets. I used to imagine when drinking their milk that I could still smell the fragrance of honeysuckle or wild violets.

The whole farm was my playground. There were no Keep Off signs, but it was an unwritten law that gates must never be left open. 'Shut that yett!' the men would shout after me. And it was the blackest of sins to traverse a corn- or turnip-field instead of using the pathway that had been left at the edge, the heidrig where one could cross in comfort without damaging the crops.

There were sturdy stone walls round many of the fields, drystone dykes built patiently, stone upon stone, by some old dyker in the past, a craftsman in his own right, and kept in repair by the shepherd who was Jack-of-all-trades and master of many. I thought him the cleverest man in the world. He could make and mend a clothes-horse or a hen-house, lend a hand at haytime and harvest, catch moles, kill pigs, fell trees, and act as midwife to the cows. But his greatest accomplishment, to my mind, was whistling through his fingers and commanding instant obedience from his collies by a few terse words.

' 'Way by, Jed! In ahint! Doon, Jess!'

When I tried it, they just turned tail and went their own ways.

'Man-lassie,' said Jock-the-herd, shaking his wise head at me, 'there's a knack in't. I doot ye'll never lairn it.'

I doubted it, too, but I still tried. Alas! to this day 'whustlin'' is not one of my accomplishments.

The farm had once been a battlefield, and lay in that debatable no-man's-land betwixt two warring countries. Only a short distance away stood the range of Cheviot hills with a winding old coach-road leading to the Border. The Carter Bar. Beyond lay enemy territory. England, where the Sassenachs lived.

> Fee-fi-fo-fum,
> I smell the blood of an Englishman.

I pictured them as a wild tribe who crept across the frontier to steal our cattle, plunder our houses, and burn our abbeys. The Scottish reivers, engaged in similar pursuits, were not to be blamed. They were merely retaliating!

When I had mastered the magic art of reading, I filled my head with bloodthirsty ballads.

> When Percy and the Douglas met,
> I wat he was fou fain.
> They swakkit swords til sair they swat,
> And the bluid ran doon like rain.

It was not easy to forget the old fighting days, for the ruins of a Border keep still stood on our hillside, though the sheep and cattle now grazed peacefully enough around it. It was here that the Scots kept a look-out in the old days, ready to light a warning bonfire when the English raiders were sighted creeping across the Border; and here I played houses as a child, with a ready-made castle at my command.

The surrounding farms had strange and fascinating names. Bloodylaws I liked best, because of its wicked sound. Our own,

Overton Bush, was plain in comparison. It was known locally as the Bush, or merely the Buss, in the old Scottish manner. Stotfield marched on one side, Falla on the other. Nearby were Dolphinston, Dovesford, Mervinslaw, and Oxnam; and away down country we could see the Eildon Hills 'cleft in twain' by Michael Scott the Wizard.

But these were far-away and out-of-reach places for a child. It was the immediate surroundings that mattered. The farm itself was a world of its own. The men who worked in the fields were called hinds and the women bondagers, in the old feudal fashion, but they were no mere hirelings; they were our friends.

The hinds wore rough jackets, corduroy breeks, tackety-boots, and leggings which they called nicky-tams. Sometimes they were tied round with binder-twine, or even with straw twisted into rope. Often the scarecrows looked better-dressed, for the men seemed to spend more time grooming their horses than bothering about their own appearance, and were for ever brushing and combing the Clydesdales' tails or plaiting their manes.

The bondagers, too, wore coarse serviceable garments, kilting up their long skirts and fastening them with safety-pins over striped petticoats. But it was their headgear, the distinguishing mark of their trade, that fascinated me and made me determined to become a bondager when I grew up. Big black straw hats shaped in Dolly Vardon fashion which shaded their weather-beaten faces from wind and sun. Sometimes they wore red-and-white spotted kerchiefs underneath, tied under their chins and half-covering their faces. It was difficult to tell who was who unless one peered closely enough under their hats. In wet weather both men and women flung empty sacks over their shoulders to protect them from the rain, making them look more than ever like tattie-bogles. But what did appearances matter? Under their trappings they were all honest, loyal and hard-working. The farm was as much theirs as ours.

Like Lucy Gray, that solitary child in the poem, I was a lone bairn. Not because I was bereft of brothers and sisters, but because I was an in-between, far beneath the regard of a superior sister four years older – a lifetime to a child – and of a brother some eight years my senior. Destined for the kirk, no less. He seemed a lordly creature who rode away each day on a spirited pony to the Grammar School in Jedburgh, mounting from the big stone at the kitchen door. The loupin'-on stane. What happened at the other end I never knew; but I often watched him cantering down the farmroad with his school-bag bobbing on his back, and wondered how on earth I would get off and on the pony when my turn came.

Later he disappeared from my ken to attend college and university at a far-off place called Edinburgh, the capital of Scotland, reappearing for the holidays more of a stranger than ever. What could he, who was learning Latin and Greek, have in common with a mere toddler? To my elders and betters I was less than the dust.

Later on, there were younger ones who came, after a gap, to fill the nest. But during these formative years I remained Number Three. Nobody in particular. A nuisance, as I was often told. It was best, I found, to get on with my own ploys and keep out of everyone's way. Except maybe Jessie's.

Jessie! How can I describe her? For many years she was the most important influence in my young life. I still think of her often, remembering her wise saws and wishing I could still turn to her for advice when in difficulties.

'What should I do, Jessie?'

'Och! juist bide your time an' things'll sort themsel's oot.'

The first sounds I can recall are the clip-clop of her clogs as she went to and fro on the stone kitchen floor. Jessie always seemed to be coming or going, never sitting still with folded hands. Her hands, indeed, were seldom empty. She was always carrying kettles or milk-pails or an apronful of kindling. Or, if she was working outside, a sheaf of corn or a forkful of hay.

Jessie was the odd-job woman on the farm, who worked as a bondager when she was needed, and at other times lent a hand in the Big Hoose. At any time of stress and trouble the cry went up, 'Fetch Jessie!' I used to run helter-skelter out to the fields where she was singling turnips or spreading dung calling breathlessly, 'Jessie, you're wanted!'

We had a succession of servant-lasses in the kitchen. Raw young slavies straight from school. Daughters of herds or hinds from neighbouring farms, they clattered clumsily about the place, dropping dishes and tumbling over pails. But they, poor things, were dim creatures compared with Jessie, and, in her opinion, had little rummlegumption.

Rummlegumption was Jessie's word for commonsense, which she herself possessed in abundance. Upright in every way, straight as a ramrod, she knew the difference between black and white but none of the subtler shades in between. A thing was either right or wrong, full stop.

Jessie had a handsome, nut-brown, gypsyish look about her, with a hawk nose, beetling black brows, and a firm mouth. The kind of face a sculptor would have enjoyed hewing out of some hard material. She made no pretence at fancying-herself-up. Her strong black hair, streaked with grey, was combed back into a firm bun and fixed with fearsome-looking hairpins which never left their moorings. She wore long skirts, high-necked blouses, and a stout apron which she called a brat. Except on Sundays when she put on 'ma good costume'.

Though her whole body seemed so stiff and unyielding and there was nothing soft in her looks or speech, I instinctively felt a sense of security when I gripped her rough hand. The Scots word lippen – to depend on – must surely have been invented for Jessie. If she gave her word, threat or promise, she would carry it out.

She used to call me 'the peerie-top' because I was so seldom still.

Although she belonged to me, I thought, Jessie had another

life. She lived with her brother, the shepherd, and her sister Joan (whom she called Joo-anne) in a cottage some distance from the others, set down by the roadside. The herd's hoose. Joo-anne sometimes emerged in her big straw hat to work as a bondager, but was more often a stay-at-home, looking after the cottage and cooking the meals. Everything was as neat as ninepence inside. 'Ye could tak' your meals aff the flair,' was Joo-anne's boast; but I was glad to see that they had a table. I also remember seeing a string of salt fish hanging outside the door and the herd's long drawers blowing in the breeze.

It was a rare treat to visit the herd's hoose and find him sitting with his stockinged feet on the fender, while Joo-anne knitted on one side of the hearth and Jessie mended his socks on the other. And never a word spoken. Once, late at night, I had to take a message to them, and was amazed beyond measure when Jessie came to the door in a long white goonie, with her hair in a pigtail tied with blue wool.

Looking back, it is Jessie who stands out most clearly in all my childhood memories; and it was she, above anyone, who did most to mould my character. Indeed, my goal was to grow up to be as good as her, and with as much rummle-gumption. It is a goal, alas! that I have never reached.

It surprised me to learn that Jessie had had a previous existence. Sometimes she would speak of her younger days when she was in service in a great house in the town, and of what the parlourmaid and 'the mistress' had said or done. It had been the one adventure of her life, away from the fold; but I had a feeling that she must have pined under all the restrictions and was happier now that she could come and go more freely on the farm.

Certainly her life was varied enough, both indoors and out. Like her brother the shepherd, she could turn her hand to a hundred tasks. I have followed her about while she singled turnips, stooked corn, fed the hens, or turned the hay; and watched her milking the cows, churning the butter, doing the ironing, baking scones, making mealy puddings after the pig-killing, or sitting with a mouthful of pins putting a patch on a pair of breeks.

Jessie was the most complete person I have ever known. In a way, she was my first encyclopedia. Certainly my first story-teller. And, though she never knew it, it was because of her that I became a story-teller myself in later years.

I used to follow after her, pleading, 'Tell me a story. Go on, Jessie!'

'Hoots! I've yell't ye them a' afore.'

'Never mind! Tell me again.'

I could have listened to Jessie's stories for ever and never wearied. Especially when she was milking the cows. I still have the little red creepie-stool on which I sat in the byre, watching her milking and listening to her tales. I often stare at it today when searching for inspiration for my own stories; and I seem to hear her voice saying, 'A'weel, there was ance a wee black-an'-white pownie . . .'

Jessie's stories were all about animals. 'Beasts', she called them; and she told them in the broad Border dialect which seemed to add breadth, depth and colour to them. Tales about cows and pigs, which she called coos and soos; and about the bubblyjock, which was Jessie's name for the turkey-cock.

She had no sooner finished one story than I begged for another.

'Tell me more, Jessie.'

'Hoots, lassie, your heid's fou' o' beasts already.'

But in the end she always gave in; and sometimes, to humour me, she would say, 'I'll gie ye a guess.' I had heard her 'guesses' so often that I always knew the answer, but I pretended to puzzle them out.

> Tammy Riddle, Tammy Riddle, Tammy rot-tot-tot,
> A little wee man wi' a red, red coat.
> A staff in his hand an' a stane in his throat.
> Tammy Riddle, Tammy Riddle, Tammy rot-tot-tot.

After pondering for a while I would hazard a guess. 'Is it a cherry?'

'Ay, that's it!'

Jessie had certain rituals which never varied. She would not give me anything without first holding it behind her back and saying, 'Nievie-nievie-nick-nack; which hand will ye tak'?' I had to choose the right or the left, and if I chose the empty hand, I got nothing!

Though Jessie used words sparingly, they were always to the point. She had a rich turn of phrase and could conjure up an old saying to suit any occasion. Often she described me as being 'as daft as a yett on a wundy day' or 'like a hen on a het girdle'. I could see myself flapping about in the wind or jumping up and down on the hot girdle beside the scones.

But she was not one for speaking for speaking's sake. I never heard her address her brother if their paths happened to cross on the farm. Occasionally they might exchange grunts or nods, but that was as far as they would go. I used to wonder what their conversation was, if any, when they sat by the fire in the herd's hoose at night.

One way and another I spent much of my early life in prison. I was a 'bad bairn', so I was told; yet, strangely enough, it was my good deeds that most often caused my downfall. I had a great desire to be helpful, but my acts of kindness directed towards human beings were seldom appreciated. So, in the end, and with no better results, I directed them towards the animals.

There were more of them around, anyway; and on the whole I felt they had an unfair deal. The bull, for example, bellowing with boredom at a closed gate. What was wrong with letting him out for a change of scenery? Or brightening up the sow's life by inviting her into the garden to smell the flowers? Or, for that matter, bequeathing my Sunday hat to the scarecrow? Not entirely out of kindness! I hated the brown straw with its tight elastic band. In any case, it looked better on the tattie-bogle than on me.

I never knew how long my sentence would last. I was just pushed through the door leading up the rickety stairs to the garret and firmly locked in, with an admonition to: 'Bide there till you behave better.'

Sometimes I sat on the stairs and considered my sins, but not for long. I could never see why I was guilty. Besides, there were so many fascinating things to see and do in the gaol. Far from being a punishment, I looked forward to my sentences of solitary confinement.

The garret was as full of junk as an Old Curiosity Shop. It had a strange musty smell till I let in the fresh air by scrambling on top of a decrepit dressing-table to prop up the skylight window. It was a precarious perch, but if I clung on and poked out my head, I could look down the slated roof and see the contents of the rone where many odd objects were stuck. Rubber balls which I had tossed up and lost for ever, arrows fired into the air from my brother's bow, hair-ribbons blown sky-high in the breeze. I was too far up to be able to reach them, but at least I knew where they were, and if ever I had wings I could fly up and retrieve them.

If I leaned far enough out I could gaze down, like God, on the whole world. It looked like a toy farm, with miniature sheep dotted about the fields and haystacks as small as thimbles. Even Jock-the-herd was reduced to a dwarf. If he came near enough I sometimes called down to him.

'Hullo-o-o, Jock!'

He would gaze up, wrinkle his brow, and call, 'Man-lassie, are ye in again? What is't this time?'

'Nothing!'

But the herd knew better. He would shake his head at me and pass by, with Jed and Jess at his heels. I could sense that, like Jessie, he was muttering, 'Nae rummlegumption!' Grown-ups never seemed to give one the benefit of the doubt.

Sometimes a cushy-doo would alight near my head and give a friendly 'Prrrrr' before flying off to freedom, leaving me to thole my sentence as best I could. Though it did nothing to reform my character, the household gaol enlarged my out-look in many ways, and certainly taught me to content myself with my own company; though I was never really alone. There was the other me inside, with whom I held long conversations and who, thank goodness, never scolded or considered I was lacking in commonsense. We got on a treat and never once quarrelled.

Time never dragged in the gaol; there were so many treasures to be discovered in the dusty corners. Discarded toys, an old wooden cradle, a pensioned-off rocking-horse, a battered banjo, a chest full of feather-boas and faded finery. Best of all, a pile of old books with their batters hanging off. Bound volumes of the *Quiver, Sunday at Home, Spurgeon's Sermons,* and a *Medical Dictionary,* with yellowed pages and f 's for s's.

I used to sit for ages in a creaking rocking-chair, shoogling backwards and forwards while poring over the old print. The words were difficult, but at least I could look at the pictures of goitre, diseased livers, and floating kidneys.

One day I came across a musty old Bible and tried to de-cipher the spidery writing on the margins. The sacred, I discovered, was mixed up with the secular. A reminder that: 'Today I gave the clocker a setting of brown eggs' was side-by-side with a comment on a sermon. 'The minister preached a good discourse. Seek and ye shall find.'

I sought and found treasure-trove between the pages. There were cuttings from old newspapers announcing births or deaths, recipes for making parkins, cures for the toothache, how to take stains out of tablecloths, a photograph of some bygone Sunday-school picnic, an envelope containing 'Baby's first hair-clipping'. And in Revelations I found a half-written letter. 'Dear Thomas, No, it must not be. My mother says we are not to meet again. So . . .'

So what? I wondered. It was like turning the pages of the past, trying to piece the jigsaw together and bring old stories to light. The hours of my imprisonment ticked quietly away and I felt no sense of loneliness.

In spite of the farmhouse being so old, there was nothing eerie or spooky about the gaol. The only thing that disturbed me, if daylight began to fail, was the presence of 'the body'. Mother and Jessie occasionally did dressmaking for the family and kept the dummy in the garret when not in use. Sometimes it stood straight, like a naked lady with no legs; at other times the body lent sideways against the wall. Once it slithered down and landed with a clatter at my feet, startling me out of my skin. But on the whole it was pleasant enough in prison, and and peaceful except for the squeaking of mice in the skirting-boards, which I found friendly rather than frightening. Sometimes they came out and played a kind of jing-a-ring amongst themselves, paying no attention to me. I just watched them and let them get on with it.

In winter the skylight window was often frosted over, and sealed so tightly with icicles that it let in little light, and I could not see to read. In any case, the garret was so perishing cold that I had to keep on the move. I blew on my fingers, waved my arms about, and ran races with myself. Sometimes I burrowed in the old chest to find a shawl or a moth-eaten fur cap to drape over my shoulders. Riding the rocking-horse helped to keep my circulation going, till one day it creaked to a standstill and refused to move either backwards or forwards.

When all else failed I could try to pluck out a tune on the banjo. On the back, some dreadful old jokes had been scribbled out.

BONES: Say, Boss, what am de difference between an optimist and a pessimist?

BOSS: De difference, Bones? De difference am that an optimist

he look after de eyes, and a pessimist he look after de feet.
(laughter)

There was no means of telling the time so far away out of
earshot of the grandfather clock in the hall, and no knowing
when my gaolers would remember to let me out. If it grew
pitch dark, I went down the rickety stairs and thumped on the
bolted door, calling: 'Let's out!' to anyone who happened to
pass. Usually they had forgotten, as I had, why I had been put
in prison. But one thing was sure, I would be back again.

The best place to make for as soon as I was free was the
kitchen rug. I would sit there eating a jammy-piece and getting
warmed through while the stir of the house went on around
me. Usually I shared the rug, and the bread-and-jam, with a
dog or cat or a bantam-cock, sometimes even with a pet lamb.
Often I could hear a cheep-cheep from inside the oven, where
a chicken – the weakling of a brood – had been put to recover,
wrapped in a piece of flannel. When it showed signs of becoming lively, it was taken out of its makeshift incubator and
delivered back to the protection of its mother's wings.

I had to keep a wary eye on the big black kettle which hung
on the swey over the fire. Sometimes it would boil over and
spit out at me till I hastily swung it to the side. Often there was
a pan of stovies bubbling away, or a dumpling being boiled
in a cloth, or an outsize pot of food for the pigs. Great quantities
of potatoes in their jackets. The soos'-meat, Jessie called it.

The pigs'-pail always stood in the back-kitchen ready to
receive any left-overs. What a strange hotch-potch of a menu
the soos ate! Stale gingerbread mixed up with apple-peelings,
crusts, carrots, treacle-pudding, cabbage-leaves, cheese-rinds;
even bits of bacon, which I felt reeked of cannibalism, though
Grumphy and Co. did not seem to mind and appeared to thrive
on such an unbalanced diet. When the pail was full it was
carried out to the pigsty and the contents poured into the
trough where eager snouts were soon routing in the mixture
till every morsel disappeared.

The stone-flagged kitchen seemed a vast place to a child. The big dresser, where the lamps stood ready for lighting, contained all the dishes and platters needed for the household, as well as drawers full of cutlery. There were other odd drawers where aprons, dusters and dishcloths were kept, and where anything lost could be found. 'Look in the dresser drawer' was an everyday cry when a key was missing or someone was searching for scissors.

A great bin with a sloping lid held sacks of meal, flour, salt, and sugar, enough to see us through a snow-siege; and a long wooden table stood in the middle of the floor at which a dozen or more men could feed at clipping-time or threshing. Six could sit on the old gaol-stool which was shoved under the table when not in use. Where it came from I never knew; it was just part of the household, as familiar as Jessie herself.

Great hams hung from the ceiling and strings of onions from a hook on the wall. There was no other adornment except a calendar advertising sheep-dip. It had splendid coloured pictures for each month. The Blue Boy, Buckingham Palace, snow-scapes in the winter months, and seaside scenes for summer.

The back-kitchen was a utilitarian place, full of pots, pans and basins, a rough wooden table, and a sink at the window where the washing-up was done. The window looked out over the untidy back garden and away down the fields towards the shepherd's cottage. Many a time I stood there on tiptoe to peer out and see if the postie was coming. He left his bicycle at the road-end before traversing the fields and climbing the fences with his mail-bag bobbing up and down on his back. What a welcome sight he was, coming as he did from the big town and bringing with him not only newspapers and letters, but, better still, all the gossip of the countryside.

From the back kitchen a door opened into the dairy which Jessie called 'the milk-hoose'. It was a cool place with wire-mesh at the window which could be left open so that the air, but not the flies, could get in. Here the milk was sieved when it was brought in from the byre and poured into shallow dishes. When the cream gathered it was skimmed off into an earthen-ware crock, to await churning. Eggs, butter and cheese were also kept in the milk-hoose, and sometimes trifles and cold puddings. Little wonder the cat was always sniffing at the door.

'If ye leave the milk-hoose door open, ye'll no' hae your sorrows to seek,' Jessie used to warn me.

The nearest thing we had to a refrigerator was the meat-safe which hung outside and was reached through the back kitchen window. Here the butcher-meat or sausages were kept and our own mutton if the herd had been killing a sheep.

We had never heard of deep-freezes or, indeed, of any of the mod. cons. taken for granted today. Jessie sprinkled tea-leaves on the carpet to lay the dust before starting to sweep with a besom. She went down on her knees to scrub the kitchen floor, and spent hours blackening the grate and polishing the fire-irons with emery-paper. Sometimes she used pipe-clay to make fancy patterns of whirls and whorls on the doorstep as a finishing-touch.

Going 'ben the hoose' meant opening a door in the kitchen which led to the hall, the staircase and the front door, with the two main rooms opening off. The drawing-room and the dining-room.

The drawing-room would have been better-named the parlour, though it had bits of grand furniture. A buhl cabinet, the piano, a large mirror taking up the full length of one wall, various nick-nacks on the mantelpiece, a beaded footstool, and a white sheepskin rug. Yet, it was small enough just to be a ben-end and could look homely when the fire and the lamps were lit. The shabbier it became the less drawing-room-y it looked.

What I recall most about the best room were the two cushions plumped up on the sofa, one in each corner. They were made of dark purple velvet, with words and pictures worked on them in bright colours. On one a langorous lady, bedecked with jewels and wearing a lovely evening-gown, lay asleep with a beatific look on her face. The words read: *I slept and dreamt that life was beauty.*

On the other cushion the same lovely lady had awakened to reality. She was now wearing a ragged dress and an apron, and in her hand she held a broom with which she was wearily sweeping the floor. The words now read: *I woke and found that life was duty.*

It had a sobering effect on me. I tried to puzzle over the meaning of it. Was life always to be like that, I wondered? And was it only in dreams that one could find beauty? I felt so sorry for the lady that I turned the awake picture wrong way round every time I came into the room, and left her to her happy slumbers.

Life must have seemed very real and earnest to the older generation, judging by a sampler hanging on the wall, painfully cross-stitched by my mother when she was a girl.

> A youth who would in life excel
> Must study, plan, and toil as well.

Could one not have a little fun thrown in, I wondered, and never mind the excelling?

The most lived-in room was the dining-room, the biggest, brightest, and untidiest, with everyone's clutter lying around on the sideboard, table, and chairs. Father's desk was here, and the safe which he opened with a key kept hanging on his watch-chain.

Inside were mysterious papers and bills over which he pored now and again with a puzzled brow. But he had no love for 'business', and sometimes pushed the papers aside, opened another drawer and brought out a strange musical instrument. An ocarina. Father had the ability to coax a tune from any-thing – a Jew's harp, a tin whistle, even a paper-and-comb. Sometimes he sat at his desk, ignoring the bills and playing the ocarina, oblivious to all else.

I liked trying out the stamping-machine on his desk. If I pressed it down firmly enough on a piece of paper, the magic address came up: Overton Bush, Jedburgh, Roxburghshire. Long before I could read, I knew the shape of the letters by feeling them with my fingers.

My mother's sewing-machine was here as well as the big bookcase and the wall-cupboard – the press – where the best china was kept: the gold-patterned wedding-cups and the good dinner-set with its great ashets, soup-tureens and vege-table-dishes. The damask tablecloths were kept in the side-board drawer along with the lace-edged teacloths to be brought out when company came.

At mealtimes the cry went up: 'Clear the table!', and there was a great shifting of ludo, snakes-and-ladders, stamp-collections, knitting, newspapers, the cat, or anything else that had landed there. A thick undercloth protected the polished surface, and a leaf at each end could be pushed in or pulled out, depending on the number of diners.

I remember the day a French polisher came to furbish up the table and how disappointed I was when he spoke in a Jedburgh accent. I had been hoping to meet my first foreigner.

The sideboard groaned under the weight of tureens, ashets, and great jugs of cream, especially when visitors were present. The food was mostly home-produced. Chickens or whole sides of mutton, if a sheep had been killed. There was always plenty of game, too, to be had on the farm. Pheasants, indeed, were so often on the menu that I used to envy folk who ate sausages and thought how rich they must be. They were a treat to us who saw butcher's-meat so rarely.

The divinity students from Edinburgh who sometimes came home with my brother for the holidays used to wallow in the homely fare, licking their lips and asking for second or third helpings of everything. It used to surprise me to see them drooling over the cream. What was so special about it? There was always heaps of it in the milk-hoose.

I was not an eater myself, except of 'rubbish'. Sweeties, if I could get them, or anything I could find for myself and eat between meals. Sitting in to a set meal, which seemed to go on for ages, I considered nothing but a nuisance, and had to be forced with many a dire threat. Usually it was, 'The bubbly-jock'll get you.' He was the creature who terrified me most – the great gobbling turkey-cock who flew at me with out-stretched wings and pecked at my bare legs.

If I failed to finish my porridge Jessie would lower her brows and say, 'Mony a stervin' heathen wad be gled o' them.' She always referred to porridge in the plural, and indeed the kind she made were so thick that they stuck to the ribs. 'Eat them up. They'll pit a guid linin' on your stamoch.'

My stomach was well enough lined with the extras I foraged for myself. Raw turnips howked out of the field and hacked into slices with the gully, stolen for the purpose. Hips, haws, and many other fruits of the hedgerows helped to ease my hunger, as did the young garden peas which tasted far sweeter from the pod than when they were cooked. Brambles, blae-berries, wild rasps and crab-apples (which we called scrogs) formed part of my outdoor diet; and I daresay I was lucky not to poison myself by eating the juicy stalks of reeds, nibbling 'soorocks', by sampling the little red barberries which grew on a bush by the burn, as well as chewing ears of corn, docken-leaves, and anything at all that looked faintly edible.

I can recall many happy hours spent sitting on a heap of bean-locusts, intended for the beasts and not for me, eating my way steadily through them. They tasted vaguely of squashed dates, and had a kind of compulsiveness about them so that I kept on eating long after they had filled me to bursting-point. Perhaps that was the way the cows ate, without knowing when to stop. Small wonder I had no appetite when faced with a plate of cockieleekie soup or a helping of stovies.

Jessie, who was never one for compliments, used to say, 'Ye're a peelly-wally object, an' nae wunner! Eatin' a' the rubbish. Wait an' see! Ye'll puzzen yoursel', an' naebody'll greet.'

2. Elders and Betters

Like the Rhode Island Reds and Minorcas who were provided with cosy enough hen-houses but seldom stayed in them, I had a great urge to get away from restricting walls. Freedom was the thing, and freedom lay outside.

Not that I wanted to be a hen. I had seen too many of them having their necks wrung, poor things. It was a higher price than I was willing to pay for being free; but if I could escape from Them, the grown-ups, I was out of the door like a shot.

If it rained, I never noticed it. Through the rose-coloured spectacles of childhood the sun was always shining. Whenever I got the chance I discarded shoes and stockings and ran bare-foot all over the farm.

Run was the word. Strange how children, with all the time in the world before them, feel impelled to rush helter-skelter at everything, urging themselves to run fast and faster, to jump

high and higher, to turn bigger and better somersaults. *Wait* is
not a word that figures in any child's mind.

I rushed all over the place, clambering on to roof-tops and
daring myself to jump down from terrifying heights. 'Go on,
fearty!' One-two-three and off I went. Jessie was right. Like a
peerie-top, I was seldom still; unless there was something
special to watch.

Running barefoot had its pains as well as its pleasures. I was
seldom free from scars. The bubblyjock and the bantam-cock
pecked at my bare fetlocks, thistles and nettles reached out to
sting me, prickly thorns and whin-bushes scratched at me as I
ran by. But what did a few wounds matter? The pleasure was
well worth the pain.

It was a wonderful feeling, climbing trees barefoot without
fear of tearing stockings or scuffing shoes. My feet were soon
as tough as leather, and I could scramble up like a monkey,
curling my toes round the branches and digging my heels into
the bark. Certainly I was nearer to nature when I could feel
the good earth beneath my feet and the long grasses swishing
against my legs. And it was bliss to walk into the burn and
guddle in the cool water, knowing that I could walk out again
without bothering to dry my feet. I grew more and more like
a wraggle-taggle gypsy and kept well out of sight of any prim
visitor, for I was no show-piece.

As for cuts and bruises they were only occupational hazards
to be taken in one's barefoot stride. I soon learned how to
doctor myself by rubbing soothing docken-leaves on my
stings, washing my wounds in the burn and tying wet handkies
round the worst of them. I knew better than to complain about
them, especially to Jessie who taught me, above all else, to be
stoical. Indeed, I felt it was wicked to be ill.

If anyone asked me – which was seldom enough – how I
was feeling, I just said 'Fine' and left it at that. Never mind the
raging toothache, ignore the bumps and bruises, forget the
thumping headache. Unless a limb was actually broken, there

was nothing the matter with me. Minor ailments were not to be discussed.

It was no use running to Jessie and saying, 'I've got a pain.' Her only reply would be, 'Weel, what aboot it? Stop girnin', an' it'll get better.' Pain was something to be borne alone, not passed on to other people. True enough, the less one thought about it, the sooner it disappeared as if discouraged through lack of attention.

Jessie did not approve of pills and potions which, according to her, sent people 'oot their minds'. Her chief remedy was a spoonful of treacle which she administered with a fine disregard for the locality of the ailment. 'Fetch the trykle tin,' she would say. Then, 'Open your mooth,' and over it went. At least, if it did no good it did no harm, and was more palatable than the greasy castor-oil which tasted worse than poison.

Sometimes, if I could not hide the fact that I had succumbed to a severe chill, I was given a concoction called toddy, made up of whisky, lemon, sugar and hot water, which I was forced to drink to the last drop before being sent to bed feeling pleasantly tipsy. I remember the bed floating round the room and the ceiling revolving. Then nothing else till I awoke with the shivers gone.

As for feeling ill herself, Jessie would never admit to such a weakness, though it was known that she suffered from a recurring ailment known as 'the bile', but she never gave in to it. When an attack came on she went about with tighter lips, took occasional sips of boiling-hot water and gave an angry thump to her stomach. Bodies were nuisances when they were not running smoothly, but the less one thought about them the better.

A tattered volume entitled *Till the Doctor Comes* was kept in the dresser drawer and consulted when anyone broke out in spots. The advice given was usually, 'Keep the patient quiet', which Jessie interpreted as 'Haud your wheesht!'

Getting the doctor was an enormous step not to be taken

lightly since he had to travel over seven miles to attend to us. He was sent for only in the most stringent cases: to remove tonsils or set a broken arm. Even then it was the doctor who received all the attention. The patient was of little moment compared with such a grand personage who arrived in a big motor-car, driven by a chauffeur, and wearing a long coat with a fur collar.

In Jessie's eyes he was equal to, if not above, royalty. A fire was lit in the bedroom for his benefit, not the patient's, and the best towels laid out. A tray was set with a lace cloth and the good china, in case he might fancy a cup of tea.

'Lie still,' Jessie warned me when he appeared carrying his wee black bag, 'an' dinna daur open your gab.'

I was much too awed to tell him my symptoms, even if I knew them myself. When he sat down by the bedside with his stethoscope slung round his neck and asked how I was feeling, I just gave the usual answer. 'Fine!' It was up to him to find out whether I had pneumonia or a broken toe.

Minor operations were performed on the kitchen table, specially scrubbed for the occasion and with cats, dogs, hens and pet lambs banished outside. The smell of chloroform mingled with the aroma of mutton roasting in the oven, and the patient floated into oblivion to the familiar sound of the herd shouting to his collies as they passed by the kitchen door.

Being kept in bed was the worst fate in the world to me. I would not have minded the measles so much or the mumps and the whooping-cough if only I could have stayed up a tree or been left in the Cockit Hat. It was the bedroom that seemed sickly, as if it was suffering from an illness. The window was tightly closed and the door firmly shut to 'keep the patient quiet'. A shoogly wee table was set by the bedside on which was placed the dreaded bottle of medicine and the equally hated glass of hot milk.

I had nothing to do but stare at the ceiling, count the colours on the patchwork quilt, listen to the muted sounds of the

household, and strain my ears to hear the grandfather clock
in the hall chiming the slow hours. I read my bound volume
of *Chatterbox* from cover to cover though I already knew it
inside-out, and even studied the uplifting text-for-the-day on
the wall-calendar. 'Blessed are the meek for they shall inherit
the earth.' What nonsense, I thought; they never would!

Years seemed to pass before the current servant-lassie came
clattering up the stairs carrying a tin tray – no fancy lace
d'oileys for me – containing a bowl of beef-tea or a plate of
milk-pudding.

'What's going on?' I asked her eagerly, as if I had been
marooned for months on a desert island. But she could seldom
think of anything better to say than: 'Nothing!'

I liked best when Jessie mounted the stair. She would sit
straight as a poker on the edge of the chair by the bedside
and tell me that the cow had calved or that the corn was
ripening. Once she brought me a sprig of southernwood from
the garden (which she called appleringie). I lay still for ages
afterwards, holding it in my hand and smelling its clean sharp
fragrance. It seemed to bring the outdoors into the stuffy bedroom and did me more good than all the shake-well medicines
in the bottles.

I tried to detain her on all manner of pretences, that I needed
a drink of water, that I had lost my book (I was hiding it under
the patchwork quilt), that the stone hot-water-bottle – the pig –
was cold. Jessie saw through my wiles and her ministrations
were rough and ready. Yet, though she wasted no sympathy
on me, I liked just to look at her and clutch at her hard hand.
She would plump up my pillows and say briskly, 'Stop
whinin'. There's mony a deid body wad envy ye.'

I lay like a deid body listening to her receding footsteps and
longing for the day when I could get up and follow her out
to the byre at milking-time.

Sometimes Jessie sang to the cows, or, at least, crooned a
tuneless little ditty.

Katy Beardie had a coo,
Black an' white aboot the moo.
Wasn't that a denty coo?
Dance, Katy Beardie.

The cows looked round at her with their large limpid eyes, mooing for more. Jessie declared they gave more milk when she sang to them. Maybe so, but it was her stories I liked best.

'Tell me the one about the wee pig with the curly tail. Please, Jessie.'

'Toots! I tell't ye that ane yesterday. Can ye no' gang awa' an' lairn to mak' up stories for yoursel', lassie?'

So I did.

Well, at least I tried; but they were poor shadows of Jessie's. All the same, it was Jessie who started me off, unknown to her, on my writing career.

I made up my first stories in the gaol and kept them in my head, since I had not yet mastered the art of writing or spelling. They were all about beasts and tattie-bogles, and when I recounted them to Jessie in the byre, as a kind of swap, she looked at me with great suspicion and said, 'Ma certies! sic an imagination ye've got. Mind! I'm warnin' ye; it'll lead ye into trouble some day.'

Maybe she was right, but I did not heed her warning. She had started me off and there was no going back. Ever since then I have been making up stories, dipping into the rag-bag of my mind and pulling out any of the tangled tales I can find there. Sometimes I come across some half-remembered saying of Jessie's and try to recall its meaning. In the course of one of her stories she described someone who 'jumped aboot like a cock at a grosset.'

'What's a grosset, Jessie?'

'A grosset? Wumman, d'ye no' ken it's a gooseberry?'

I was by no means the only audience in the byre. Some cocks and hens wandered in at intervals, and a semicircle of cats sat on their tails with cracked saucers in front of them, awaiting their share of the milk. They were of all shapes and sizes: black-and-white, tortoiseshell, ginger, None of them had names. Jessie just called them all 'Cheetie-pussy', take it or leave it.

My own favourite was the lame white kitten who always sat next to me and had a special way of mieowing up at me as if she was talking. I would answer her by mieowing back, and many an animated conversation we held about goodness-knows-what.

'Ye're a daft pair,' Jessie used to scoff, digging her head into the cow's side in disgust.

One dreadful day the little lame one went missing at milking-time. The others were all in their usual places: the tortoiseshell, the black tabby, the ginger tom, and the rest. But not a sign of my favourite. I ran all over the place hunting for her, up haystacks, in the granary, under the reaper, even in the hen-houses. But she was not to be found and my heart was broken.

'There's plenty mair,' Jessie told me with cold common-sense. But none like the little lame kitten.

It was the next day when I was still hiccupping with grief that Jessie said briskly, 'Stop mumpin', wumman. Open that drawer an' bring me oot a duster.'

I listlessly pulled open the drawer – and out jumped the lost kitten with a duster clutched in her claws. What a reunion we had! I gave her a saucerful of milk and she looked up at me between sips, mieowing out her story. She had jumped into the drawer when someone had left it half-open, fallen asleep amongst the dusters and been imprisoned when the drawer was shut.

Farm bairns, of course, cannot afford to become too senti-mental over animals, or squeamish about the realities of life and death. I had enough gumption to realize that pigs were fattened to be killed, that lambs would be made into chops, and that even the proud bubblyjock would end up on an ashet at

Christmas. All the same, I could never bring myself to join in
the chase of a young cockerel due for execution, and always
looked the other way when its neck was wrung. It was terrible
to think of it alive one moment and dead the next.

'Ay, but ye'll help to eat it, nae doot,' Jessie would say as she
was plucking off the feathers.

Yes! I would eat though I would not kill. There was nothing
consistent about my feelings. But somehow roast mutton or
boiled fowl bore so little resemblance to the live beasts that I
could forget my finer feelings when the creatures were cooked.

Pet lambs were a different matter, and caused me much
heart-rending when the shepherd took them away to the
slaughter. Often I had fed them like babies from a bottle. They
were usually the weaklings of the flock, with a lame leg or a
wry neck. I remember one that looked over its shoulder all
the time, a black curly creature who followed me wherever
I went, always looking backwards.

Like the cats, none of them had names. I played with them
like toys, but suddenly they would shoot up to an alarming
size, big enough to knock me over when I was a toddler. I
used to sit astride one of them and ride it round the farmyard
like a pony, though it is fair to say I had no control over it and
was forced to go where the lamb listed. Many a tumble I took,
too, as it swerved round corners, chased by the turkey-cock.

The only time I took a scunner at the herd was when I saw
him sharpening his knives preparatory to killing the pig. A
murderer, I thought him, and ran miles to be away from the
terrible squealing. I did not come back till long after the
dastardly deed had been done and the body of Grumphy
washed, scraped, disembowelled and hung up in the shed so
that all the blood could drain out of him.

There was great activity in the kitchen where my mother
and Jessie were busy cleaning out the puddings and stuffing
them with oatmeal before boiling them. They also concocted
mysterious little parcels, called faggots, out of the innards:

chopped liver mixed with onions and herbs, covered with a fatty membrane for some part of the pig. Indeed, almost every part of the deceased animal was edible. Even the lugs and the trotters were singed at the fire before being cooked, and the head made into 'potted-heid'.

Later, there would be a great cutting-up and salting-down of the carcase which provided many a succulent meal for the household. And not only for us. The cottagers, the herd, the postie, and the vanman went off with parcels of spare-ribs, surely the tastiest part of the pig. Similarly, we received our share when the herd or the hinds killed their own sows. Give and take was the thing.

I soon forgave Jock for his bloody deed, especially when he presented me with the pig's bladder, dried, cleaned, and blown up like a great opaque football. The blether, he called it. He tied a long string to it so that it could float in the air, and I played with it till it burst, sparing only a few pitying thoughts for poor Grumphy. By the time the great hams were cured and ready for eating I had forgotten he ever existed.

Sometimes the hinds coming home from the fields would hoist me up and set me on the back of one of the workhorses. It was a perilous position. I felt a sense of terror mingled with excitement as I clung to Prince's rough mane as he clopped his way into the yard, jingling his harness and making straight for the horse-trough. It was touch and go whether I would land in the water head-first or if I could slither off in time to save a drooking.

Often I followed the men into the work-stable and watched them settle the horses into their stalls before feeding them. The Clydesdales seemed to be satisfied with an unchanging diet of corn, varied only occasionally with hot mashes in winter. It seemed as unpalatable to me as the cattle-cake which the stirks were given as an extra; but 'each to his ain taste' the hinds told me before locking the stable-door and going home to their own suppers.

I used to feel sorry for the horses left in the dark during the long winter nights, and wondered what they did to pass the time.

'Naethin',' said Tam, when I broached the subject to him.

I found it so difficult myself to do naethin' that I felt sure the horses must have their own ploys. Sometimes late at night I could hear them stamping their feet. Were they quarrelling, I wondered, or maybe dancing their own version of the Highland Fling?

My sister was a lady. She told me so herself, time and time again. She also told me I was the opposite and must have been left on the doorstep by a tink.

No running wild for her, no tumbling about on haystacks, no imitating the herd's broad accent. When visitors came she could always be relied on to appear neatly dressed with not even a hair-ribbon missing.

I admired her from a distance, like looking up at a star; but I knew I could never reach such heights of primness, so I gave up the struggle and continued on my rag-tag-and-bobtail path. Who wanted to be a lady, anyway? I would sooner have the herd call me 'Man-lassie'.

Elders were strange beings, never doing anything wrong and with no one to scold them, even if they did. Maybe I would learn sense, too, when I grew up, and feel as superior. But what a dull prospect it seemed.

My father was a kindly man who did not want any trouble. He would turn his head away from problems rather than face up to them. Anything for a quiet life.

Sometimes he dandled me on his knee and made his handkerchief disappear up his sleeve like a magician. Or he would sing me a song.

> 'There's one two three four five six seven eight
> funny little kids at home.

Two tom-cats and a she-cat, too,
An old poll-parrot and a cockydoodle-doo.
There's a half-bred dog with his ears cut short,
   and a great big fat strong wife.
With a lot like that you can eat your hat,
If I don't lead a very merry life.

Father had a funny-bone and was an entertainer *manqué*. And yet, not all that *manqué*, for he was in great demand as a 'comic' at local concert-parties around the district. I used to hear great tales of the Darkey Troupe he had got up (it was he who was the boss of the banjo in the garret) and of the difficulties they had had in making up their faces and keeping the blacking from dripping on to their collars.

One night they had been given a great ovation – so they thought – in the town hall, and responded by bowing repeatedly to the enthusiastic audience, not realizing that the captain of the rugby club had appeared on the stage behind them, proudly displaying the trophy his team had won.

One of the songs they used to sing was a tongue-twister. Father had it off pat, and could sing it all the way through at great speed – faster and faster – without ever once slipping up.

Swim, Sam; swim, Sam; swim, Sam.
Show them you're some swimmer.
Swim like the snow-white swan, Sam,
You know how the snow-white swan swam.
Six sharp shivering sharks are going to snap your limb.
But a swim well-swum is a well-swum swim,
So, swim, Sam; swim, Sam, *swim*!

I never saw the Darkey Troupe – it had been disbanded before I came along – but later on I was sometimes taken to a draughty village hall where Father was appearing as top of the bill. The rest of the programme usually consisted of anyone who could play the fiddle, however badly, and a man or a woman singing straight songs, 'Caller Herrin!' or 'Auld Robin Gray,' with accompaniments thumped out on an untuned piano.

When Father came on the discords did not seem to matter. He always brought the house down, and though I had heard his patter often enough before, I could still laugh at his antics and call 'Encore!' with the best.

There were times when I had difficulty in recognizing him, for he always dressed up for his parts. Sometimes as a coalman with a sack slung over his back ('Coals! Coals! Coals for everybody in the toon!') or as an old wifie, wearing one of Jessie's long skirts and a straw bonnet he had found in the garret.

I can remember, too, the rehearsals that took place in the parlour at home when Father got up a play. It had to be very simple: a kitchen-comedy in broad Scots, for the caste was not accustomed to high-falutin' speech or fancy acting. But on one unfortunate occasion there was an English character in the play. I could never understand why the old man who played the part shouted 'Ba! Pasha!' at intervals, till many years later I read the script and saw the words printed as 'Bah! Pshaw!' My father never had the heart to hurt anyone's feelings by correcting their pronunciation; and in any case the audience did not seem to mind.

I was once roped in myself at a tender age to act the part of a page-boy. What play could that have been? I had nothing to do except wear a tunic over a pair of fancy breeks and bow in front of my father. When the moment came I was pushed on to the stage and stood there bewildered, forgetting to bow, till Father said something funny, not in the script. Whereupon the audience roared with laughter – why, I never knew. I just gave a quick bow and got off the makeshift stage as fast as I could, ending my career before it had begun. It was better fun sitting in the front watching the others and mouthing their words, 'Ba! Pasha!' and all.

Though Father was a comic, he was more of a public funny-

man than a private one. He was a gregarious creature and liked
to be in the midst of a company, setting them all laughing.
But he seemed to find it embarrassing to talk face-to-face with
his family, as, indeed, many parents do. If I met him out and
about on the farm, it was like Jessie and the herd. We never
knew what to say to each other, hardly even 'Hullo'.

I admired him greatly, and later on in life would have liked
to get to know him as he really was. Not just as 'Father'. But
I never did. The only letter I ever received from him was signed
'Yours truly'. Often I longed for a word of praise from him.
Maybe he would have liked one from me, too; but I could
never have told him how I liked him. *Love*, of course, was not
a word to be bandied about. Feelings, in most Scots households,
are still kept bottled up.

My father was a man of many talents. He had a great
facility for all kinds of games and sports. He had been a runner
and hurdler in his youth. Now and again he rode to hounds,
and was an excellent shot, a first-class golfer, and a champion
billiard-player. Like all Borderers he was an enthusiastic
follower of rugby. The only thing he had no particular interest in was, strangely enough, farming. It was his father who
had decided his career and pushed him on to the land. But he
was essentially a town-laddie, brought up in Jedburgh and
educated at an academy called the Nest, where he learned a
smattering of this and that, including German, but nothing
about farming.

Nevertheless he did his best to get to grips with his acres. It
was a mixed farm, and though some of the seed fell on stony
ground, his crops were not always bad nor his kine lean. Like
all farmers, he had his good and bad years; and I never knew
whether we were rich or poor. The main thing was, I could
always mooch a penny from his pocket to spend at the sweetie-
shop.

Father was popular with the men and often took his place
beside them in the fields, rolling up his sleeves at haytime or

harvest, and forking with the best. But he was happier when he could get away to the market or the sales and see something of the outside world. To be a farmer's boy was not enough for him. He had many an *alter ego*.

> I'm John James Ebenezer Hezekiah
> Peter Henry Zachariah,
> John James Brown.
> Don't you know me? Go on!
> Then you will very soon,
> For I'm John James Brown,
> The chocolate-coloured coon.

This was one of the Darkey Troupe songs he used to sing.

The hinds called him the boss, or the maister, and had a great respect for him without being in any way subservient. I thought my mother was very familiar when she addressed him as John.

They were a well-matched pair, for she, too, liked entertaining and being entertained. Sometimes she sang duets with him and played his accompaniments at the concerts. In her youth she had taught in a school in the town and knew nothing of country life till my father drove her home in the gig on their wedding-night. But, with Jessie's help, she soon found her feet and turned the bare farmhouse into a home. She became an excellent cook, learned how to rear chickens, and, most difficult of all, how to cope with the isolation.

I remember her as soft and fair, easier to communicate with than my father, and with an imaginative way of describing some incident so that her stories – though in a different way from Jessie's – became alive.

Once she went on an expedition to Edinburgh and came back with her head full of a play she had seen. *Mary Rose*. She went over it all, scene by scene, calling out 'Ma-ary Ro-ose!' in an eerie voice, completely carried away as if she was living the part herself.

At that time my father and mother must have been quite young, but anyone above ten seemed elderly to me. Jock-the-herd was a hundred, in my eyes, and Jessie reached away back to Biblical days. In fact, I once asked her if she knew David.

'Wha? D'ye mean Davy Scott?'

'No, the one who killed Goliath.'

'Him! He was afore ma time.'

I could not visualize Jessie as a lassie, playing with a skipping-rope. Although she did not know David, she often talked in tones of great reverence of 'the auld Queen'. Victoria the Good. She had been queen when Jessie was young, and though Victoria was long since dead and gone, I heard about her so often that I almost felt we were related. Not that I would have been fit to clean the auld Queen's shoon, as I was told many a time.

'*She* wad never hae left a dirty plate,' Jessie scolded me, looking grimly at my half-supped porridge. 'She wad think black burnin' shame o' hersel'.'

The auld Queen was perfect. Indeed, the whole world had gone to pieces – to babbyrags, Jessie said – since Victoria ceased to reign. '*She* wad hae sorted them,' she said fiercely when the newspapers reported some misdeed of the government. 'It's a wunner she's no' birlin' in her grave.'

I used to picture the auld Queen whirling round in her shroud till her crown came tumbling off her head.

For a long time I thought Queen Victoria had something to do with tea, for her picture was on the caddy which sat on the mantelpiece in the herd's hoose, a fierce-looking old lady wearing a wee lace cap. Albert was on the other side but he always had his face to the wall, for though he, too, was good, Victoria was better. Jessie handled her reverently every time she brewed the tea, and made sure the caddy was carefully dusted every day so that the auld Queen would look spick and span.

Though I found it easy enough to converse with Jessie and the herd, I found it more difficult to make contact with the hinds who all seemed like giants to me, though their names were short enough: Wull, Tam, Bob. They called me 'the wee ane' and treated me with amused tolerance, even when I asked daft questions.

'What's that you're spreading on the field, Wull?'

'Dung!'

'What's dung, Wull?'

'Och, it's just a kind o' – perfume. Can ye no' smell it?'

Sometimes they sent me running back to the house – anything to get rid of me, I expect – with a message for my father.

'Awa' an' tell the boss the binder's broken doon. Ask him to bring oot a spanner.'

'What's a spanner?'

'Hoots! just gang an' tell him.'

But by the time I had run back to the house, though I tried to keep the message in my mind, it had become so fankled that my father had to go the the field to find out for himself.

Elders and betters never made mistakes. This, I thought, was one of their most unendearing traits. To be grown-up and sensible, I considered, must be a terrible fate; never to run barefoot, never to hold imaginary conversations with a tattie-bogle or to believe that cats could speak. Old people's conversation was dull and matter-of-fact. Politics and prices seemed to be their main topics, or what the weather was likely to be to-morrow.

It was the same with the animals. The young lambs would kick up their heels and play cuddy-loup-the-dyke while their staid mothers looked on disapprovingly. The hens clucked crossly at their straying chicks, the cows turned lofty looks on their calves when they ran races, and even the cats called their kittens to heel if they showed signs of being too playful. They were all, in their own ways, saying 'Don't!'

So – it was best to have as little as possible to do with grown-ups. They were queer creatures, I thought, and it was safer to watch them from a distance.

3. The Travelling Folk

Anyone who ventured up the bumpy farm-road must inevitably be coming to visit us. Where else could they be going? There was nothing beyond but hills and more hills.

All the same, strangers did come and surprise us by chapping at the kitchen door – waifs and strays seeking food and shelter for the night. At that time there were many more tramps, tinkers, and gaun-aboot bodies on the roads; and these wanderers were never turned away from our door. My father was known to have a soft heart, and the word must have been passed round to say that free lodgings were available. Sometimes we saw mysterious marks at the road-end and wondered if this was the tramps' code.

Often they arrived at the gloaming, so weary that they were not particular where they slept; in the barn or in one of the outhouses, any place where they could lie down under cover. But one old crone, called Nellie, who always smoked a clay-pipe, had a preference for the byre as her bedroom.

'Put me aside the coos,' she pleaded. 'They mak' grand het-waitter-bottles.'

Nellie was always given permission but warned that she must not smoke because of the danger of fire; and sometimes I would be sent round to see if she was obeying instructions. Not her! I would find her sitting on the hay with her bundles around her, chatting to the cows and puffing away at her pipe.

'Ye'll no' tell your faither, wull ye?' she would say in a wheedling voice, giving me a crafty sidelong glance.

I never did, though I had a guilty feeling that if Nellie set the place ablaze it would be my fault and I would get what-for from my father whose heart was not as soft as all that.

The cows seemed pleased enough with Nellie's company, and she always gave them a fond farewell in the morning as well as a parting word of advice. 'Behave yoursel's noo! Be guid coos, an' Nellie'll be back to see ye again afore lang. Ta-ta!'

I welcomed the sight of any strange face and often acted as go-between, carrying out the tramps' tea and pieces to them when they sat on the bench near the kitchen door easing their feet in their cast-off boots. While they ate I studied their wrinkles, their matted hair, their hands ingrained with dirt, their tattered garments, and listened to their unfamiliar talk, for some of them had come from over the Border where the Geordies lived, and others from down-country where the accent was different from ours.

All of them carried untidy packs and bundles. Some trundled old prams in front of them containing all their wordly goods, consisting mainly of rags rolled up in newspapers. Yet they were always begging for more.

'Hae ye ony auld claes or a pair o' shoon? See! I've nae soles left. I'm walkin' on ma uppers.'

Some even looked longingly at the tattie-bogles who were often better-dressed. Yet they were not all as poor as they pretended. One biblical-looking couple, whom we christened

Jakob and Martha, used to drive up the road in style in a pony and trap. The skinny pony was let loose in a field where it rolled over and over, kicking up its heels, while Jakob and Martha came shauchling into the house carrying a bag clinking with golden sovereigns for my father to keep in his safe for the night.

Time and again he tried to persuade them to put their money in the bank. No! They trusted my father but would have nothing to do with banks. Yet they, too, though they were carrying hundreds of pounds around with them, would beg like paupers for a pair of shoes or an old overcoat.

Some of the tramps had goods to sell. They opened their packs on the doorstep and showed a paltry display of ribbons, boot-laces, elastic, safety-pins and cheap combs. My mother always bought something for the sake of giving them a few coppers; but they were never satisfied. Always they overplayed their hands, mooching for more till our pity ran thin.

They could always conjure up a cough, real or imaginary, and put a pathetic whine into their voices when begging. Or they would send their smallest snivelling child to the door with a tear-jerking story, while the rest of them hid round the corner. Sometimes the waifs would be brought into the kitchen to get warmed in front of the fire, but they never stayed long. I remember one of them staring around like a frightened animal and crying 'Let me oot!' as if terrified he would be trapped.

The girls all seemed to be dressed up for Halloween in old shawls and trailing skirts. I used to gaze at them in envy and long to share their wraggle-taggle way of living. But it was difficult to make friends with them. I once approached a small tousle-haired bairn and said, 'Come on and play.'

Play! She shook her head and retired behind her mother's tattered skirt. The child knew how to beg but not how to play. All she wanted from me were the shoes off my feet and the ribbons off my hair, and she was welcome to them.

The gypsies were always willing to tell fortunes by way of recompense; but I was not so willing to have my hand held in theirs while they foretold fame, fortune, and a handsome husband. In any case, I was already bespoken. My intended (not that he knew it) was Jock-the-herd, who had fortune enough for me.

All the same, it was safest to keep on the right side of the Romany clan in case they ill-wished us. There were frightening tales, true or false, of crops failing, cows going dry, and hens stopping laying as the result of a gypsy curse. We were always faintly uneasy until we had seen the last of them straggling down the road.

I never remember being frightened of any of the tramps no matter how strange they looked or how eccentrically they behaved. I sat beside them on the bench, watching them re-packing their bundles and listening to their conversation. Not that it was directed to me. They were all great talkers-to-themselves and kept up long private running-commentaries which only they understood.

Jessie used to drag me away.

'You'll get beasts,' she said fiercely; and indeed I sometimes did get beasts, which resulted in terrible tussles with a small-tooth comb and in paraffin being poured over my locks.

Strangely enough, it was the most refined of all the tramps who caused us the most trouble, a true gentleman-of-the-roads, dressed in a top hat and an old waterproof tied round the waist with string. He was known as Yorkie, no doubt because he originated from Yorkshire where his father had been a parson. Yorkie, too, had been destined for the church; but he had been 'over-educated', so he told us, resulting in a weakening of the brain. He was full of high-flown talk, so disconnected that it was difficult to make head or tail of it. But Yorkie was quite content to be his own audience.

Unable to lead a settled life, he had taken to the roads with a rough-haired tyke at his heels and an old fiddle under his arm.

All the year round he roamed about the countryside, roaring out his demands for food and shelter. There was nothing subservient about him. Yorkie did not beg; he ordered.

We could hear him long before we saw him, coming shouting up the road in that eerie half-light of the gloaming. He would play a few screeches on the fiddle and then knock loudly on the kitchen door with his stick. He had originally come to the front door until firmly forbidden. If his summons was not instantly answered he came straight in, sat down and helped himself to any food he could find on the table without a by your leave. Yorkie always gave us the impression that he was a cut above us.

My father knew how to handle him, and would soothe him down if he was in a tantrum, then light a lantern and lead him off to the barn or one of the sheds. But sometimes in the dead of night we could still hear him shouting in his sleep. The only time we ever locked the doors was when Yorkie was about.

One night he came roaring up the road long after the household was in bed. My father called out of the window to him, telling him that he could go and sleep in the strawbarn. Yorkie went off, mumbling to himself, and lay down in the dark. But not for long. Soon such an uproar broke out that it wakened us all up. We could hear Yorkie yelling at the pitch of his voice, his dog yelping in a frenzy, cocks and hens cackling in alarm, and a pig screaming as if its throat was being slit.

When my father went out to investigate, he discovered that Yorkie had lain down on the straw in the barn, not knowing that an old sow had burrowed underneath. No sooner had the tramp settled himself and dropped off to sleep than the sow heaved herself up, tossed him in the air and ran grunting from the barn, looking like a white apparition.

'The place is haunted! There are devils here! I'll never come back again, never!' roared Yorkie, hurrying away down the road in the moonlight with his dog barking at his heels.

But, of course, he did come back, time and time again. Haunted or not, he made good use of the farm and its hospitality, till at length we heard he had found more permanent shelter in the churchyard.

Our most welcome visitor was the postie, a cheerful man with a bright red face and a bristling moustache. He wore a waterproof cape, carried a large canvas bag, and came at varying times of the day, depending on how long he had been detained at his previous calls. He had cycled the seven-odd miles from Jedburgh, left his bike at the herd's hoose and walked diagonally across the fields to reach our door.

The postman suffered from flat feet, and little wonder. As well as cycling on the main road he had to tramp many a mile across rough moorland, often to deliver only a postcard to some outbye shepherd's wife. Sometimes he was the only human being the cottagers saw for days on end; and it was not the mail that mattered to them as much as the verbal messages he carried. Greetings from one isolated family to another, as well as the latest clash of the countryside.

And not only verbal. The postie was obliging enough to act as message-boy if he got back to town before the shops closed for the night. He would fetch medicine from the chemist, waiting patiently till prescriptions were made up, take clogs to the cobbler, match wool, carry samples of curtain-material, even take false teeth to be mended.

The postie wrote down his transactions in a small black note-book with a stub of pencil which he licked and rubbed against his moustache to sharpen the point. Then he ticked the items off methodically once they were completed. He was never known to refuse, or to complain of the trouble it must have taken to trudge round the shops after completing such a hard day's work. Even sorting out everybody's dribs and drabs of money and giving them back the right change must have been a nuisance.

The postie himself would never take any money for his pains.

The only way to repay him was in kind. His bag was often bulging with gifts from grateful customers, and sometimes they overflowed into the inside pockets of his cape as well. He must have had many an unsteady ride home in the darkness, laden with pots of jam, home-made scones, fresh butter, eggs, and spare-ribs.

I liked the days when the postman had time to come into the kitchen for a cup of tea. He dumped his bag on the table, slung off his cape, and sank into a chair, bending down to loosen the laces in his boots. Then, having eased his feet, he gave a sigh of relief, took a long gulp of tea, and reached out to undo the straps of his postbag.

The mail was done up in little bundles tied with string. There was always *The Scotsman* for my father. Nothing, of course, for anyone as insignificant as me, except maybe at Christmas when the postbag was more than ever like Pandora's box.

'Naethin' but accoonts,' he would say apologetically to my father. He preferred handing out something cheerful, like a coloured postcard of Portobello. 'It's the minister's wife. She's enjoyin' hersel' a treat on her wee holiday.'

The postie knew everything about everybody, but we knew little about him. Where did he live? Who cooked the spare-ribs for him? Had he a wife and family to go home to, or any life of his own after plodding round the shops at night? He never talked about himself. Just licked his pencil, rubbed it against the bristles of his moustache, and asked, 'Ony messages?' before retying his laces and slinging his cape back over his shoulders.

I had a feeling he had been invented for us. He was 'our postie' and that was his only role in life.

When the turnips were ready for singling and extra hands were needed the Paddies mysteriously appeared. Goodness knows where they came from or what they did for the rest of the year. They arrived out of nowhere, rough-looking men with thick Irish brogues, knocked at the kitchen door and asked to see the boss. My father went out to speak to them, made some sort of bargain with them, and hired them on the spot if he liked the look of them.

The Paddies were paid by the piece, so much per row of turnips singled, and worked hard from early morning till darkness to earn as much money as possible while the going was good. They kept themselves to themselves, seldom mingling with the other men, and slept in one of the sheds, calling at the kitchen door for their 'meat'. Jessie handed out great pots of tea, bowls of soup, and hunks of ham, but was wary about entering into conversation with them. 'Kittle-cattle,' she called them.

On Saturdays after they had been paid the Paddies disappeared down the road and we never knew whether they would come back again. Sometimes they walked all the way to town and spent their money in an orgy of drinking, reappearing bleary-eyed and penniless on Monday morning to start all over again.

Kittle-cattle or not, the Paddies brought a bit of excitement to the place with their colourful language and their songs about Mother Machree and Dublin's Fair City.

Amongst our itinerant visitors was a strange little man who came to dig drains on the farm and set up residence in the bothy near the lambing-shed. He did for himself and left messages at the farmhouse for the goods he required, always in verse.

> Bread, if you please,
> A nice piece of cheese,
> Some raspberry jam,
> And a big hunk of ham.

I thought his poems were even better than Anon's and wondered why, with so much talent, he remained a mere drainer.

I wondered a lot of things as I watched the travelling folk coming and going. What was the world like beyond the confines of the farm? Would I ever be able to spread my wings and see for myself? The only way would be to put a pack on my back and go off, like the rest, to sell ribbons and laces.

The best way to see the world, I discovered, was to go by gig, though our main means of transport was shanks's pony. We thought nothing of walking the two miles to church and back, or trudging long distances across the hills to visit another farmstead. Or even on occasions plodding the seven-odd miles to Jedburgh, taking adventurous short-cuts by scrambling down steep screes, traversing unfamiliar woods and fields, and finally following the river Jed.

In the days before my father bought his first car (known as 'the motor') the gig was our only other means of locomotion. This, though, was not always quicker, depending on the mood of the pony, how long it took to lure her down from the hill, and how reluctant she was to be yoked into the trap. It depended, too, on how temperamentally she behaved once she finally set off, and how often we had to get down to open and shut gates across side-roads. It was best to leave a leeway of an hour or so one way or the other.

There were two gig-ponies. Flora, the white one, and Ginger, the chestnut. I liked Flora the best, perhaps because of her imperfections. Ginger was just a horse but Flora was a friend.

She had been 'in the family' for years and would turn her head at the sound of our voices. If she was in a placid mood she would come running to meet us. But she knew fine, when my father went off to fetch her with the bridle in his hand and a pocketful of corn, that she could lead him a dance; and she often did.

If she was in a capricious mood it was like a game of cat-

and-mouse. Sometimes Flora was to be found in the cow-gang cropping the clover or rolling over in the soft grass. At the sound of approaching feet she would gather herself together, jump the fence and canter off to the hill. Often the herd and his dogs had to come to the rescue and round her up; but there were times when she came meekly enough, neighing with pleasure and nudging against my father till he gave her some corn and slipped on the bridle.

The gig had been pulled out from the cart-shed and dusted down ready for the road, to the annoyance of the bantams who used it as a roosting-place, and Teenie – the lame hen – who never laid an egg anywhere else. Once she went all the way to Hawick with us before we discovered her, and flew out into the High Street to the surprise of all concerned.

The fluff and feathers were shaken off the seat-cushions, the lamps given a hasty polish, and finally Flora was backed in between the shafts, protesting as usual. But once the harness was in place and the bit between her teeth, the pony's nostrils began to quiver and she had to be restrained from taking off like a rocket before we mounted to our places.

I always had a backward view of the countryside, for the gig was like a jaunting-car with back-to-back seats, and it was only grown-ups or important folk who sat in front with the driver and had a straightforward look at the landscape.

It was strange to watch everything receding into the distance, the farmhouse growing smaller and smaller, the fields moving away backwards, and Jock-the-herd reversing out of sight. If we went quickly enough the trees seemed to be dancing a kind of waltz to the rhythm of the wheels and clip-clop of the pony's feet, whirling round and round and stretching out their branches to each other.

It had such a dizzying effect that it was best not to give way to such flights of fancy. I had to keep alert and cling on to avoid being pitched head-first into the ditch, especially when Flora swerved suddenly round a corner. Many a time I have landed sprawling on the road, with bruised knees and a frightened feeling of being left behind.

'Wait! I've fallen out!'

If my shout was not heard I had to run after the gig in the hope of catching it up on the next steep brae when the pony slowed down and the occupants got out to walk. But if the gig was spinning smoothly and swiftly along the level, it was well out of my reach in no time. I remember sitting disconsolately by the roadside, feeling abandoned by the world, till at long last my father, having discovered I was missing, turned the pony round and came back to retrieve me.

The jolting and joggling was good for the digestion, if nothing else.

'It fairly shoogles up your internals,' Jessie used to say on the few occasions when she could be persuaded to 'go for a hurl'.

We got plenty of fresh air, too, for there was no hood to cover us. We tucked an old tartan rug round our knees when the weather was chilly, and huddled under a waterproof sheet when it rained. Flora, too, had a macintosh cover, and in summer sported a straw sun-bonnet of sorts and ear-muffs to keep off the flies.

It was the pony who set the pace. My father hardly needed to do any driving for Flora knew every twist and turn of the Border byways; and on the main road to Jedburgh, when she reached one of the half-dozen drinking-troughs by the roadside, we had to await her pleasure if she was feeling thirsty. Flora knew exactly where each one was situated and would swerve to the side to drink her fill.

Sometimes she gave a hungry whinney and had to be fed from her nosebag before condescending to set off again. Or she would suddenly take a fancy to some fresh grass on the verge and stop for a nibble. When my father urged her to get a move on she turned a reproachful look at him. 'What's the hurry?' she seemed to be saying. 'I'll get a move on when I'm ready.'

But if Flora was in a frisky mood and there was a level stretch of road ahead she would take to her heels and speed like the wind. I felt like a bird flying backwards through the air. If my hat blew off I just let it go. Goodbye, hat! Unless by chance it landed on a stucking-post and we could pick it up on the way back. My mother, sitting forward, wore a long veil which she swathed over her hat and tied firmly under her chin.

When the pony was in an easy-osy mood there was ample opportunity to see the scenery and have a word with anyone we met on the way. Our friend the postie, the roadman, the gamekeeper, or the minister. Even Yorkie, the tramp.

If anyone wanted a lift and there was room in the back I had to squeeze to the side to accommodate them. In my day I have shared the back seat with many an odd customer. One was an Ingan Johnny whose bicycle had broken down. He sat holding the bicycle on his knee, spoke in a strange tongue and, naturally enough, smelt strongly of onions. He presented me with a long string of them as a parting gift, slinging them round my neck like beads.

If we came face-to-face with another equipage on a narrow road there was a great deal of jockeying to the side before we could pass without the danger of the wheels becoming entangled. Meantime, the horses rubbed noses and my parents had a chat with the occupants of the other carriage. If it was a gypsy caravan, Flora would bare her teeth and toss her head at the piebald pony till both of them reared up and we almost toppled over.

On some side-roads leading to hill farms there were as many as half a dozen gates across the road which we had to open and shut. No one ever volunteered for the job. I always hoped it was not my turn but it often was.

When I was given the order I reluctantly jumped down, clambered up the gate and had a great struggle with the sneck. Sometimes it was tied with binder-twine, and often in knots which had to be unravelled before I could swing the gate open. When the gig was driven through, the gate had to be shut again and the string retied, for even other folk's yetts must never be left open.

How I loathed those gates! If there was another within sight, it was not worth the bother of getting back into the gig. I just walked on always hoping that this time the operation would be simpler. I got to know the good ones and the bad ones, and wished Flora would jump over them, gig and all.

On a steep hill the pony would sometimes go on strike and come to a complete standstill. We had to get down and walk on in the hope that Flora would follow.

'Tak' nae notice an' she'll come,' Jessie would say. 'Fashious cratur!'

It was not so much the scenery that attracted Jessie's attention when she was riding in the gig as the washings hanging out.

'That's a guid clean wesh,' she would comment approvingly. Or she would remark on the crops and the gardens. 'See thon thristles. It's high time they were howked oot.' She kept a keen look-out, too, for any bondager she could spot working in the fields. 'Thonder's Aggie. My! she's gey stiff. She's gettin' past it.'

Travelling with Jessie opened my own eyes. She noticed so many things. Different curtains on a cottage window, a pipe-clayed doorstep, a new tattie-bogle in a field, a broken fence, a 'whummled' sheep lying on its back struggling to right itself. My father always pulled Flora to the side, got out of the gig and climbed into the field to turn the sheep right-way-up.

It was a great thrill to be promoted to a seat beside the driver and see the road stretching far in front of me. Better still to have a turn at the reins, though Flora took little heed of my driving and went where she wanted, snorting with derision if I attempted to tug her to the right when she pre-ferred turning to the left.

If we were on our way to the big town it was strange how

Flora always settled down and stopped her capers when we approached the outskirts and saw Jedburgh Abbey in the distance. She always held up her head when we reached the High Street and stepped smartly out as if she knew people were watching. She was not so pleased to be left in a strange stable while we went to do the shopping, and always greeted us with whinneys of delight when we returned laden with parcels ready for the journey home.

Sometimes we had to light the gig-lamps and drive home in the darkness. It was eerie watching the oncoming lights and wondering if we could pass without the wheels touching. I used to stare at the sheep's eyes gleaming like little flashing beacons from the fields and try hard to keep my own eyes open, for if I drowsed off I might lose my balance and tumble out.

Often Flora drowsed, too. Her pace grew slower and slower till my father called out: 'There's the road-end! We'll soon be home.'

As we swerved into the home-straight Flora seemed to scent the corn in her own stable. She tossed her head, whisked her tail and cantered up the last lap, snorting at every step and coming to such a sudden standstill at the door that once more I was in danger of being pitched out.

If we arrived home when it was still daylight the pony could hardly wait to be freed from the shafts before taking to her heels and making straight for the cow-gang. Without waiting for the gate to be opened, she took a running-jump and leapt over. Then down she lay in the grass and rolled over in an ecstasy of freedom. The gig was pushed back into the cart-shed and left once more to the mercy of Teenie and the bantams.

How often I used to watch for a sight of the gig-lights, if I was left at home. I would stare for hours out of the dining-room window into the darkness, hoping for a first glimpse of the flickering far-away lights. I could tell by the way they were bobbing up and down if Flora was trotting and how long she would take to reach the kitchen door.

Sometimes, if we were all at home, the cry would go up: 'There's a light coming up the road,' as if it was coming up by itself. Then we would all run to the window and speculate. Was it a bicycle-light or a lantern? Could it be Jakob and Martha coming to seek shelter for the night, or maybe a neighbouring farmer paying a visit in his horse-and-trap?

There was never any curtains drawn in the house. Coming home in the darkness it was comforting to see the welcoming lamplight shining softly from the windows as if the house was alive and waiting to say, 'Come in!'

As often as not it was Jessie who acted as our Leerie and lit the lamps. It was not everybody, certainly not me, who could be trusted with the task. The wicks had to be evenly-trimmed, kept low at first, then gradually turned up, but not too quickly in case the glass globes cracked. The lamps must never be set in a draught or placed on an unsteady table where they could easily be knocked over. Above all, they must be watched carefully every now and then to make sure no accident had happened.

'Tak' a keek at the lamps,' was Jessie's constant cry; and she kept me running upstairs and down to see if all was well. If anything happened, it was my fault.

'Silly lassie! Ye've reeked the place oot!'

The lamps were in different shapes and sizes and were placed in strategic positions all over the house. Some had fat globes and some thin. One was tinted pink to give a rosier glow. There was a big reading-lamp, the little one for the landing, an even smaller one for the window-ledge at the turn of the stair, a special one for the bathroom, and bigger brighter ones for the kitchen and back-premises.

Altogether they transformed the farmhouse, softening everything and taking away its shabbiness. But there were still some pools of darkness left, and it was wisest to hurry past them when going from one place to another. The eerie shadows thrown up on the walls and ceilings could sometimes look like prehistoric monsters.

If lighting the lamps was an art, cleaning and filling them was a major operation. This ritual took place relentlessly every morning when they were all set out on the kitchen table. They looked a formidable lot which would have made even Aladdin's heart sink. Alas! no genii appeared no matter how hard we rubbed them.

Jessie rolled up her sleeves ready for action and made me follow suit, if I was in one of my helpful moods, with many a warning to, 'Ca' canny wi' the globes.'

The great thing was to breathe on them in the right places and to have enough clean dusters handy. But it was a tricky job especially with the narrower funnels, and many a scolding – and skelping – I have had in my day when, in spite of all my care, the worst happened, resulting in broken glass, and like as not, a cut finger.

We kept spare globes in the house but never enough. It was a tragedy if we ran out of them during the dark winter nights when we were snowed-in and could not get replacements. Worse still if we ran short of paraffin; then there was nothing for it but to resort to candlelight.

Not that I minded. I liked the candles better. For one thing, they were easier to light, and though they gave a different dimmer glow, they had their own charm. I loved lying in bed watching the fantastic shadows flickering across the ceiling. Cinderella's coach on its way to the ball. The horses and hounds in full cry. A witch flying on her broomstick. It was like being at 'the pictures'. The pattern shifted and changed till someone in authority came and snuffed out the candle, taking away the matches in case I should be tempted to relight it.

Apart from indoor lighting, there were the lanterns used by the men outside. The hinds carried them from their cottages to the work-stable on dark mornings; and at nights, looking from my window, I could follow the herd's progress as he went through the fields during lambing-time. The lantern-light wavered up and down like a will-o'-the-wisp with every step he took. I could tell when he was climbing a dyke or if he had laid down the lantern to attend to a new-born lamb.

Jessie, too, took a lantern with her when she went to the byre to milk the cows in the dark days of winter. Many a time I used to carry it for her and set it down in the right position so that she could see to do the milking.

In the strange half-light the byre took on an unreal atmosphere, and sometimes I dozed off on my stool with the cats sitting at my feet. In my dreams I could hear the heavy breathing of the cows, the swish of their tails, the milk streaming steadily into the pail, and Jessie's voice coming and going as she told me one of her stories.

'A'weel, ance upon a time there was a wee coo wi' a crooked horn . . .'

What a transformation when we finally installed our own 'electric' into the farmhouse and steading. The whole place came alive and we saw into dark corners where no light had penetrated before. But it was a long time before Jessie could be induced to discard the lamps. She did not take kindly to the new harsh illumination, no matter how handy it might be.

'It's no' natural,' she declared. 'Forbye, I've a feel'n' it'll blaw up ony meenit.'

Whenever she turned on a switch, which she did very gingerly, she gave a shudder as if waiting for the explosion, and was never happier than when our installation failed as it did only too often. Out came the lamps once more, and Jessie was triumphant.

'See!' she said, turning up the wicks, slowly and carefully, 'ye can aye lippen on a lamp.'

I thought the full moon gave the finest light of all. Not only that, it was the best barometer. Jessie and the hinds could tell, just by looking at it, what the weather was likely to be next day. If there was a fuzzy halo round it – a brough – Jessie would say: 'I see there's a bruff roond the mune. That means snaw the morn.'

And sure enough the moon was never wrong.

4. Willingly to School

At the ripe old age of four and a half I set off to become a mixed infant at the village school two hilly miles away.

'Ye'll be nae miss,' said Jessie heartlessly; but I knew by the way she buttoned me into my new coat and tied the ribbons firmly at the end of my pigtails that she might miss me just a little bit. Not that I was gone for ever. I would be back later on in the day with the new look taken off my coat and my hair-ribbons lost and gone for ever.

I walked there and back except on the first day. As a special treat and in order to break me in gently I was driven there in style, sitting forward in the gig beside my father. My school-bag contained a new jotter and pencil, and, more important, my dinner-piece. There were no school-meals, not even a kettle to boil on the open fire in the classroom, so I always took a medicine-bottle full of milk. *One spoonful twice daily. Shake well.*

It was a one-teacher school. Edgerston School it was called, after the little community that sprawled around Edgerston House, which really was a Big Hoose, hidden away in the woods. Here the laird who owned the estate lived, when he was not away in London looking after his business interests. He was greater than God, we thought, though on the few occasions when we met him he spoke with such an upper-class English accent that we could scarcely understand a word he said.

The school was presided over by an omnipotent being, only a little lower than God, who lived in the schoolhouse next door and was known as the master before his face and Auld Baldy-Heid behind his back. Not that he was all that bald or all that old; but he had a heid all right, and certainly knew how to knock the learning into ours.

He did it the hard way by taking out the leather strap – the hangman's whip – first thing in the morning and warning us we would get what-for if we did not behave ourselves. I got what-for many a time, not so much for bad behaviour as for being late in the morning.

It was easy enough for Auld Baldy-Heid. He had only to open his garden gate and walk a few steps to the school. But I had to set off hours before he rang the bell. In winter I left home in black darkness and often the light was fading again before I returned home in the late afternoon. I felt like the wee moudiwart in Jessie's story, never seeing the daylight.

It was difficult to time the journey with so many diversions on the way. Even before I had walked a few yards down the road a dozen different things might have happened. Often I had to turn back and chase home a stray animal who had wandered after me. A pet lamb, a puppy, a calf, the lame kitten, a bantam-cock, even the pig; all were guilty of following at my heels.

At the cottages Mrs Thing – Tam's wife whose name I never knew – was usually out pegging up the washing. Sheets, aprons, goonies, and her man's long woollen drawers. Another Mrs Thing who lived next door – Wull's wife – was vigorously shaking her rag rug. I seldom saw her except in a cloud of dust. They both stopped and looked at me, since anything was better than nothing, but they seldom said more than: 'Ye'd better hurry, lassie, or ye'll get the tawse.'

I put on a spurt but there was no knowing how soon another delaying incident would happen. I would hear the clip-clop of a Clydesdale behind me, and one of the hinds would hoist me up and give me a ride on a workhorse on its way to the smiddy to be shod. If I stopped to watch the operation time trickled away and I would have earned the master's wrath when I finally reached the school.

Sometimes a sheep would run out of a field and the herd would shout to me over the dyke: 'Man-lassie, see if ye can weir in thon yowe,' an operation which could easily take another half-hour.

When I finally left the farm road-end I had a frightening feeling of being cut off from everything familiar. That is, until I reached the lodge-gates and saw Mary-Anne who lived there like someone in a fairy-tale. Her cottage looked like a little gingerbread house with diamond-shaped windows made of spun sugar. Goody Two-Shoes or Little Red Riding Hood might have felt at home in it.

Mary-Anne opened and shut the gates when the laird's carriage drove through, and spent most of the day speaking to her hens. She was always out feeding them when I passed, holding the corn in her apron. She had names for every one of them as if they were real people. Maggie, Mary, Mrs Broon, Jemima, and Wee Rascal who had a bad habit of laying away.

Mary-Anne spoke to me, too, as if I was a hen, but she fed me on something better than corn. Sometimes she gave me a jammy-piece or a home-made rock-bun which kept me going till I turned into the big road and the diversions multiplied.

This was the main road from Edinburgh to Newcastle, which

had once been the old coach-road. I had to keep well into the side for anything might be passing – a horse-and-cart, a motor-car, a lorry, a road-roller, even a gypsy caravan. By now I had reached the half-way mark. Camptown.

In spite of its grand name, Camptown was hardly even a village though doubtless it had been a Roman camp in bygone days. Now it was only a handful of houses, one of them being the local policeman's.

The bobby seemed to spend most of his time digging in the garden (looking for clues, I imagined) but now and again he donned his uniform and went cycling round the countryside to rendezvous with a policeman from another district. What did they discuss so solemnly as they stood leaning on their bicycles at the cross-roads? There was a great dearth of crime in the district. Seldom even a chimney went on fire. It was rumoured that one of the sheds in the bobby's backyard was 'the gaol', but if so I never heard of anyone being shut in it.

The most important place in the little row of cottages was the shop which was a combined general store and post office. A Jenny A'Things. It looked the same as the rest, with peony-roses and candytuft in the little garden in front, except that it had a few sweetie-bottles in the window and a bell that tinkled when the door was pushed open.

The shop was run by a plump comfortable-looking woman, like a pouter-pigeon, called Bella. She came 'ben the hoose' from the kitchen in her carpet-slippers when she heard the bell, and went round behind the counter to serve her customers.

It was not by any means every day that I was one of them; but now and again I was given some money to buy a jotter or a rubber and told to keep the change which seldom amounted to more than a penny. But a halfpenny could buy riches in Bella's, and could even be divided into two lots at a farthing each.

The difficulty was choosing between present joys and lasting pleasures. A bar of chocolate-cream was gone in a jiffy but hard toffee could be sucked for hours. Bella made it herself and broke it into pieces with a little hammer before putting it into a three-cornered paper poke which she twisted with a few deft flicks of her fingers.

Bella also sold postal-orders, pins, needles, pirns, mustard and boot-polish, amongst other things; but it was her sweeties that interested me most. Sherbet-bags, pandrops, black balls, sugar-ally, liquorice-allsorts, and dolly-mixtures. What a wealth to choose from!

There was a strange word in faded lettering outside the door. CONFENCTIONARY. I never knew what it meant or that it was wrongly spelt. I just thought it must be Bella's name. Bella Confectionery.

Another of the cottages was my half-way house where I called in every morning to see one of my grannies. My other granny lived in a bigger house in Jedburgh, but she was always in bed and I saw her only rarely on my visits to town, propped up on her pillows and wearing a mutch on her head.

She made me repeat the catechism as I stood by her bedside. 'Man's chief end is to glorify God and enjoy Him for ever.' As a reward, she would fumble beneath the bedclothes and present me with a coin. Never a silver one, though she was said to be 'rich'. A penny or a halfpenny was enough for gabbling the creed.

My other granny was no more lavish – she had little enough money to dole out – but at least she always let me have a dip into the sweetie-tin. It stood on the mantelpiece beside the china ornaments, with a picture of a shaggy dog on the lid. The tin contained an assortment of boilings, but there was no picking and choosing. I had to put my hand in, pull out the first I touched, always hoping that two might have stuck together, and then shut down the shaggy dog lid.

Granny's joints were stiff with rheumatism, so she often had an odd job waiting for me to do. A pail of water to empty, some sticks to bring in, or the top of the wardrobe to dust. Sometimes I had to thread a needle for her, for she was always losing her spectacles, and often I carried messages for her in my school-bag. Eggs, butter, ham, or scones from the farm.

I could have stayed happily with her all day and enjoyed myself fine, pottering about, if she had not looked at the wag-at-the-wa' and warned me that it was high time I was on my way.

When I left Camptown I was in foreign territory with a long stretch of empty road in front of me before I reached the most frightening part of the journey. The Dark Woods. This was a steep incline so thickly wooded on either side that the branches met across the road, letting only a little light filter through even in the sunny days of summer.

No one ever dawdled through the Dark Woods. There were too many eerie sounds to be heard on each side, and sometimes even worse, an ominous silence. I had heard tales, too, of ghosts lurking behind the trees, and was always afraid I might meet Yorkie there.

Once (but how would anybody ever believe me?) I did meet something strange and terrifying on that dark road. A dancing bear led on a long chain by a rough-looking swarthy-faced man. I stared in surprise, and shrank into the roadside to let them pass. The man said something to me in a guttural voice and the bear reared itself up and pranced about on its hindlegs before padding away after its master.

I never said a word about it; it was too strange and unlikely a thing to mention. But later the word went round that a dancing bear had arrived in Jedburgh.

'I've seen it!' I told Jessie excitedly; but she shook her head at me. It was something I was making up. If I had seen it why had I not told anybody before? It was too difficult to explain to grown-ups.

On windy days the wind soughed and sighed through the Dark Woods. Twigs snapped suddenly, mysterious creaks and crackles came from behind trees, scurrying feet could be heard as rabbits bolted into their holes or a weasel darted across the road, baring its teeth. A hundred unfriendly creatures lurked in the depths of the woods. Even the birds seemed to be screaming abuse and cawing threats.

It was a relief to emerge into bright daylight and see the Promised Land in the distance. Edgerston; the manse, the church, and the school. But there was still a long trudge ahead and many more obstacles on the way. Sometimes I met in with the gamekeeper, a great bearded man who looked like Moses in my book of bible stories, except that he did not carry a gun below his oxter or keep a ferret inside his game-bag.

The gamey was a great philosopher and talked to me as if I was a sensible human being, not just a silly lassie. He was greatly interested in the heavens and what lay up there. Not just God, but the people who lived on the planets and would maybe come down some day to visit us. I nodded my head wisely and said 'Uh-huh!' and as a reward he sometimes let me have a keek at the ferret.

Now and then I got a ride in Wat-the-Baker's cart but that did not speed up the journey for there were so many stoppings and startings while Wat delivered pan-loaves, gingerbreads and cookie-buns at the cottage doors. He gave me the reins to hold while he did his transactions, counting out the coins and tying them up in a little leather pouch. He was no better at arithmetic than I was, and we sometimes spent ages puzzling out the difference between fivepence-three-farthings and a shilling. As a reward he gave me stale cookies to eat or a meat pie that had crumbled to pieces.

One of my regulars was Auld Chuckie-Stanes, the roadman. Maybe he had another name but if so I never knew it. Often he would be sitting on a heap of stones by the roadside chipping away at them with his hammer. When he had amassed a big enough pile he shovelled the chips into holes in the road; and his great moment came when the big road-roller arrived with

its tar-boiler and went puffing and snorting backwards and
forwards to roll the stones firmly into place.

I loved the smell of the tar and the way it clung to the soles
of my buttoned boots as I went stickily through it, instead of
having the gumption to walk round and avoid it. I left marks
all the way to school, like Robinson Crusoe's Friday did on the
sand.

Auld Chuckie-Stanes called me the wee scholar and was
always anxious to hear my lessons, particularly my poetry. I
felt foolish standing before him on one leg staring at the sky
for inspiration and reciting, 'I have a little shadow that goes
in and out with me.' Worse still were the death-and-glory
verses we were forced to gabble at school. 'Not a drum was
heard, not a funeral note.' At the tender age of five I had to
stand up and declaim, 'Shoot if you must this old grey head,
but spare your country's flag, she said.'

Auld Chuckie-Stanes thought little of my repertoire and
taught me much livelier verses.

> Rainy rainy rattlestanes,
> Dinna rain on me.
> Rain on Johnny Groat's hoose
> Far ayont the sea.

Perhaps the truth was he liked to recite himself, and would
lay aside his little hammer while he gave me verse after verse
about the Laird o' Cockpen who was prood and great, and
about the King who sat in Dunfermline toon drinking the
bluid-red wine.

I liked 'Wee Willie Winkie' best.

> Wee Willie Winkie rins through the toon,
> Upstairs an' doonstairs in his nichtgoon.
> Tirlin' at the window,
> Cryin' at the lock:
> 'Are a' the bairnies in their beds?
> It's noo ten o'clock.'

It sang in my head to such an extent that I sometimes repeated it by mistake at school when I ought to have been burying Sir John Moore at Corunna.

The greatest thrill was to get a ride in a real gypsy caravan, covered with green canvas and drawn by a prancing pony. Usually it went swaying past me, but now and again it slowed down and I would be pulled into the back where I sat with my legs dangling out beside a squad of dark-skinned children.

The pots, pans, and pails rattled as we jogged along, and the gypsy man and his wife, sitting in front, spoke to each other in a tongue I could not understand. The children sitting beside me pulled off my hair-ribbons, fingered the contents of my school-bag and confiscated my dinner-piece. Sometimes they gave me a few clothes-pegs as a fair exchange.

As we neared the school-gate I was hopeful that the gypsy man might whip up the pony and steal off with me over the hills and far away. What an adventure that would be! But he never did. I was dumped, ribbonless, on the road, and away they went without a backward glance, leaving me to face the master's wrath.

It was a bonus if I reached the school before the bell stopped ringing, but it seldom happened. My heart gave a stound of relief if I saw some other late-comers scurrying into the playground, and could dodge in behind them. Maybe a shepherd-laddie who had walked long miles across the hills, or one who had cycled across the Border from England. But it was not easy to escape Auld Baldy-Heid's watchful eye.

'What's your excuse?' he would thunder at me when I slunk into the classroom, tousled and breathless.

'Please, sir, I haven't got one, sir.'

No use telling him about the pet lamb or the baker's horse or any of the other diversions on the way. There was only one fact that counted. I had failed to turn up in time to call out 'Present, sir!' when he was marking the register.

Some of the other stragglers were glibber with their ex-
cuses. True ones, too.

'Please, sir, I was helping with the lambing.'

'My mother's expecting, sir.'

'Please, sir, I broke out in spots.'

'Please, sir, I had to wait till ma granny mended ma breeks.'

True or false, no matter! We were all given a taste of the
hangman's whip and took our punishment stoically enough,
tugging down our jersey sleeves as far as they could go, to
take the brunt of the blow. It was all part of the process of
being educated.

But for a peerie-top like me the worst part of being at school
was sitting still, without being able to get up and jump round
the room when I felt restless. On the first day I had taken a
rubber ball with me. When I brought it out of my school-bag
the master said darkly, 'What are you going to do with that?'

'Stot it!' said I, surprised at such a daft question, and began
stotting it there and then on my desk. But I was soon shown
the error of my ways and gradually my wings were clipped,
like everyone else's.

It was worse in many ways than being in gaol, but it had its
compensations. Suddenly the world began to grow bigger and
I discovered the satisfying joys of learning.

Soon after going to school I found my first friend. Two
friends, in fact; and had my first encounter with death. Real
death, not just Grumphy the pig.

The first of my friends was a big dark-haired girl called
Kate. She had something of the look of Jessie about her, fierce
and strong, with a grip like a vice when she caught hold of me.

To begin with she was my enemy. We had nothing in
common except that we were forced to sit side-by-side and
share the same inkwell. She was a foreigner who came cycling
over the Carter Bar every day, and how could I forget that her
ancestors had fought so bitterly with mine?

For a long time we kept up the old feud, taunting each other when the Battles of Bannockburn or Flodden were mentioned in a history-lesson.

'Sassenach!' I used to hiss at her.

'Scot!' she spat back, making it sound like a bad word.

At last our own battle came to a head one day in the playground. All over a pencil. Kate discovered that mine had *Made in England* printed on it.

'See!' she said triumphantly. 'You Scots can't even make your own pencils.'

'It's a rotten one!' I said, and flung it at her in a temper.

One moment we were fighting with words, the next with fists. It was another Flodden for me. I lost the battle and won my first black eye.

It was a beauty and lasted for weeks. The strange thing was, having got rid of our spleen, Kate and I became firm friends. At first I had an uneasy feeling that I was being a traitor, fraternizing with the enemy. But after a while I forgot Kate was English. She was just a lassie like myself.

Being so much bigger and stronger, she became my protector. She would push anybody out of the way with a blow that sent them spinning, re-plait my pigtails when they came adrift, tie my laces, rub out smudges on my jotter, and whisper the answers when the master asked awkward questions about arithmetic.

At the midday break we sat on the playground wall overlooking the master's garden and exchanged our dinner-pieces. Her medicine-bottle contained home-made lemonade, far more refreshing than the milk in mine. Even her bread-and-cheese tasted different and her gingerbread was dark and chewy, with a crunchy crust on top almost like Bella Confectionery's toffee. Funnily enough she preferred my barley-scones and the shortbread I was sometimes given for afters.

It was a long time, though, before I ventured over into enemy territory to visit her, but when I did I discovered other

edible delights. Singin'-hinnies hot from the girdle and oozing
with butter; ham cut as thick as steak and fried with pancakes;
tasty faggots, and home-made bread spread with honey.

I was surprised to find that she lived in a house more or less
like mine and that the English were quite civilized. Not a war-
cry was heard nor a battle-axe seen; and I escaped unscathed to
my own side of the Border without a drop of blood having
been spilled. I began to wonder if the old stories had been
true.

In wintry weather the Carter Bar was often impassable and
Kate would be missing from the school, snow-bound on the
other side. Sometimes she came over on the snow-plough, and
one day when she was storm-stayed, and could not get back
again, she came home with me for the night.

We did our home-lessons together, made toffee, and played
snakes-and-ladders in the lamplight. Meantime the old book
about the bad Border reivers was lying unheeded on the table.
Neither of us bothered to look at it; it did not seem to matter
any more. The only battles we fought were friendly ones, and
we felt it a pity that our ancestors had not solved their quarrels
over a game of tiddlywinks.

Before long I became bi-lingual in a kind of way, trying my
best to imitate Kate's Geordie accent. She called me 'hinny'
and taught me songs about Blaydon Races and the 'Fishy in the
Little Dishy'. In return I introduced her to 'Rainy Rainy Rattle-
stanes' and the 'Laird o' Cockpen'. But we kept off the Border
ballads, just in case; it was safer not to stir up the old embers.

Kate taught me many things, amongst them how to 'go
a bike', though hers was too big for me and I could not reach
the seat. But I persevered till I could pedal away in a standing
position, and Kate patiently picked me up every time I fell off.
It did not do the bicycle much good, but I was as proud as
punch at having achieved a new skill.

There was a communal boneshaker at home but it was a
man's bike, and I kept hinting that it would be great if I had

one of my own; but my pleas fell on deaf ears. What was wrong, Jessie said, with shanks's pownie?

Kate sometimes came a cropper herself and arrived at the school with bruised knees and torn stockings. Often I helped her to straighten the handle-bars and to light the little lamp when she had to cycle home in the darkness. It seemed a long lonely way for one so young, but Kate was not afraid of anything, bogle or human being, and, like Jessie, taught me a great deal about how to be self-reliant.

So now I had a friend. It never occurred to me that I could have two. I imagined everybody had only one, like one head. What would I do with another? But one day a new family came to live in the one big house in Camptown, the factor's house for the laird's estate. They, too, were foreigners, having come from a far-off country called Wales; and I wondered what colour they would be and if they would speak words we could understand.

They were just human beings. The youngest of the family was a small girl called Gwen, as frail and pale as a lily. She waited at her gate for me each morning and we walked up the road together to the school. It was she who made the first approach.

'Will you be my friend?' she asked me straight out one day when we were going through the Dark Woods.

I stopped and stared at her in embarrassment. It was like getting a sudden proposal of marriage. I never thought folk talked like that, putting their feelings into words. But the little Welsh girl had no such reticence.

'I like you. I want you to be my friend,' she insisted, clutching at my arm.

'Away!' I said, shaking her off. 'I've got one already.'

But she had put the idea into my head, and soon I had the same protective feeling towards her as Kate had for me. Indeed, if the truth must be told, I grew far fonder of Gwen than of

Kate, and was desolate on the days when she was not waiting for me at the gate. Sometimes I would see her white face at the window, and she would wave her thin little hand at me like a lady in a story-book.

It was a short friendship. Gwen was delicate and often absent from school. Many a day I saw the doctor's grand car with the chauffeur draw up at the gate, and heard whispers that she had a strange ailment called consumption, which caused her to flare and flicker like a candle. Before long her light went out. She dwined away, as Jessie put it.

Sometimes her mother invited me in to tea. She, too, was gentle and languid-looking. Even the food she provided was delicate compared with the hearty farmhouse fare: dainty sandwiches, fairy-cakes, and paper-thin biscuits. Gwen nibbled at them like a little mouse, while her mother looked on anxiously, feeling her daughter's fevered brow and urging her to take another sip of milk. Sometimes she looked at me as if comparing me with the invalid, and I felt ashamed of my appetite.

When winter came Gwen grew quieter and paler and began to cough a great deal. Sometimes she would cling to me on the road and gasp to get her breath back. I had no idea what was happening, but I shortened my steps to fit hers and did not try to hurry her.

At school she never joined in the rough-and-tumble games of the playground but stood shivering in the porch, her hands icy cold. Sometimes I would rub them for her, and try to shield her from rampaging boys bombarding us with snowballs. I longed to inject some life into her limp body and some rich red blood into her veins, but did not know how to do it.

Then for days and days she was missing. I stood at the gate looking hopefully up at her bedroom window; but I saw her only once more, wrapped in a white shawl, feebly waving to me.

Was it the next day that the blinds were drawn? It was the
doctor's chauffeur who told me, 'The lassie's deid,' and I went
on my solitary way to school, dragging my feet and wondering if the lump in my throat would ever go away.

When the master read out the register and came to Gwen's
name I said out loud, 'She's dead.'

There was a horrified silence in the classroom, and then the
master came over to ask about it in a gentler voice than usual,
before scoring her name off the book. But I just shook my
head and continued to say, 'She's dead.'

For a time I was a kind of heroine, being the first to break
the news. We had a half-holiday on the day of the funeral,
but there was nothing to rejoice about. I picked hundreds of
snowdrops and made a little cross for Gwen's grave and have
hated the sight of the flowers ever since.

Gwen's mother gave me one of her dolls, dressed in Welsh
costume, as a keepsake; but I did not play with it. I put it away
in a drawer and forgot about it, but I never forgot Gwen.

There were other more robust bairns whose steps sometimes
fell in with mine on the way to school. Boys in clumping boots
and thick rumpled stockings; girls wearing hand-me-doon
coats often too big or too small for them. The boys were
destined to be herds or hinds and the girls servant-lasses. Few of
them wanted higher education or indeed any education at all.
It was a waste of time when they could be out in the fields
doing practical things.

What on earth did we talk about? We were no great con-
versationalists, yet we always seemed to be saying something.
Quarrelling mainly, hitting out at each other with our school-
bags or engaging in long pointless arguments.

'I did not!'

'You did sot!'

'Did not!'

'Did sot!'

Sometimes we jumped in and out of the ditches or strayed over fences and played hide-and-seek, forgetting the existence of the school-bell. Or we kicked a stone up the road, passing it from one to another with our feet to keep it on the go. Occasionally a real quarrel would break out, ending in fisticuffs, tears, and torn jerseys; but we never kept it up for long. Our common enemy was Auld Baldy-Heid.

School-bairns, or indeed bairns of any kind, are great boasters, claiming feats of daring beyond the bounds of possibility. We tried to impress each other with improbable tales of having fought dragons, wrestled with wild beasts and chased away ghosts. Strange how quickly our bravery vanished the moment we were faced with the master's tawse!

One laddie called Bob could beat us all at bragging. He claimed that he could fly.

'Go on then,' I urged him one day. 'Show us.'

It was not as easy as that, he told us. He would have to start from a high place and jump off. 'All right,' I dared him. 'Climb up a tree and start from there.'

One day in the Dark Woods he did it. Bob's take-off was impressive; so was his downfall. When he fell flat on his face at our feet we feared he had killed himself and that we – or I, more likely – would be punished for it; but he was only stunned. When he got up and recovered enough breath to speak, he muttered, 'I forgot ma wings.' All the same, he was less boastful for a day or two.

There were times when I had the unenviable task of taking a new pupil, one of the hinds' bairns, to school for the first time, until he found his own feet. The one who gave me the most trouble was Wee Wullie. I thought him a nuisance, and so he was; a snotty-nosed, snivelling child who ran away across the fields if I took my eye off him. I had to chase after him and round him up like a collie-dog while he whimpered, 'I dinna want to be learnt.'

We were all learnt whether we wanted or not, by the time

the master was done with us. Goodness knows how he managed to juggle with such a mixed batch of pupils, all at different ages and stages and all crammed into the one small classroom. But he did it, his one aim being that we should all pass the Qualifying, which would take us on to the Grammar School in Jedburgh, if we were so inclined. And still he found time to put his feet on his desk and read *The Scotsman* at some point during the day, keeping the hangman's whip in evidence and giving us baleful glances over the paper now and again.

I used to sit and stare at him, wondering, as I often did about grown-ups, if he had ever been young and daft; but I could never visualize him in short trousers playing cuddy-loup-the-dyke.

From the pupils' point of view, the one-teacher one-classroom school had its advantages. Thirty or more children were all crammed in together; and though we were split, more or less, into age-groups, we could not fail to become involved in the other lessons going on around us.

Those who were still at the-cat-sat-on-the-mat stage could pick up some miscellaneous information from the top classes. Long before I had mastered the four-times table I knew about the Wars of the Roses and the source of the Nile. On the other hand it was maddening when we reached the top class to hear the infants gabbling 'Ring-ting! I wish I were a primrose', while we were trying to get to grips with vulgar-fractions.

Sometimes we found ourselves mixed up with the wrong class, answering questions that were not directed at us. It was a hitty-missy way of learning, yet we all managed to scrape through the exams and put up a good enough show when that dreadful ogre, the inspector, came to put us through our paces. For days beforehand the master frightened the life out of us with dire threats of what would happen if we failed to behave perfectly in the great man's presence. Our pockets were searched for sweets, catapults, mice, bools, and other extraneous items; and we were warned that we would get made into mincemeat if we as much as whispered during the inspector's visit.

The truth was, he was coming as much to assess the teacher as to inspect the pupils' work. It was surprising to see Auld Baldy-Heid looking apprehensively out of the window, straightening his tie, tidying his desk, and hiding *The Scotsman* out of sight, as if he feared he might be punished himself. How we would have enjoyed that, if only it had happened!

We were drilled to spring to our feet the moment the inspector appeared and greet him with 'Good morning, sir,' in unison. I once got the strap for putting up my hand and asking, 'Please, sir, what'll happen if he comes in the afternoon?'

When he did arrive he was as mild as milk. A jokey wee man with a twinkle in his eyes, who took a cursory look at our jotters, asked a few easy questions and told us we were doing fine. Fancy! not even a cross word. Somehow we felt cheated when he went away with a cheerful wave of his hand and not a drop of blood spilt.

The master was so relieved that he lit his pipe, sat down with his feet on the desk and had a good read of the paper, leaving us to our own devices.

But Auld Baldy-Heid was not often in such an amiable mood. His temper would suddenly burst into flame, and we were seldom left sitting in the same place for long, for he had a habit of bawling: 'Go to the bottom of the class, you donkey!' No easy job, since we had to shuffle past each other at the narrow desks and were never too sure which was the top and which the bottom.

But we had our compensations. Being allowed to clean the blackboard was a great reward, the peak of every child's ambition. How powerful we felt, rubbing out sums and spelling. Sometimes, in a fit of bravado, we would draw a chalky face on the clean board, an unflattering resemblance of the master. Or even compose verses which we thought witty beyond words.

> Lang legs, splay feet,
> He aye mak's the bairns greet.

Another gem which used to convulse us with giggles was far cleverer than any in the poetry-book.

> The master's a brute,
> With his baldy heid.
> Bang! bang! bang!
> Shoot him deid!

How we hated him! Yet deep down how we loved him, in spite of his angry outbursts. He knew fine how to get round us. He had only to put away the strap, give us one of his rare smiles and say: 'What about a story?'

'Oh yes, sir; please, sir!'

Infants and older pupils alike listened avidly to the master's stories, for he had a rare talent for telling a tale. He could transport us far from the dingy schoolroom with stirring stories of the clans, or legends about ugly ducklings and toy soldiers. Sometimes he gave us a bible lesson, telling us about Jonah and the whale or Daniel in the lions' den.

We could see it all happening as the master marched up and down in front of us, waving his arms about and acting out the parts. It was like a one-man show at the theatre, and we sat entranced, hanging on every word.

Then suddenly he would drop us back to earth with a bump. Grabbing the chalk he turned to the blackboard and began to write out some sums; and life became real and earnest once more.

Now and then, to complete our all-round education, he would give us a singing-lesson, using a long cane to point out the doh-ray-me's on the blackboard; but more often he used the pointer to rap us over the head when we strayed off the tune. It was no use protesting, 'Please, sir, it wasn't me, sir.' If we were taking communal lessons we had to settle for communal punishment.

I could never get the hang of the doh-ray-me's.

'Just sing *la*,' the master roared at me, rapping my head with the pointer.

We all la-la'd our way through simple tunes: 'My Bonnie Lies Over The Ocean' and 'Clementine', with the boys groaning and grunting a few paces behind. As there was no school piano, Auld Baldy-Heid gave us a note to start us off, but it was often so high or so low that we ground to a standstill half-way through 'O My Darling.'

Sometimes he made us sing a dreary ditty called 'O Who Will O'er the Downs So Free?' It was enlivened only by the phrase 'To win a blooming bride', which we took to be a bit of bad language, and giggled behind our hands every time we sang it.

What we dreaded most of all were the times when he divided us into groups and made us sing a Round, setting us off at different times as if we were running a handicap race. 'Come, follow' was his favourite, but not mine. It usually ended in an inextricable muddle, like a tangled piece of knitting.

'Idiots!' roared Auld Baldy-Heid. 'You're all as dumb as dykes.'

He was not so dumb himself. Occasionally he segregated the sexes and took the boys off to his garden for a 'digging lesson' while his wife came in to take control of the girls and try to teach us sewing. She never succeeded in my case. My fingers were soon covered with blood where I had pricked myself, and how I longed to change places with the boys!

When we were let loose at the midday break we rushed out into the open air like bumbees from a byke, and tore about from one side of the playground to the other, jumping and shouting to give vent to our pent-up spirits. We swallowed our pieces as quickly as possible and then got on with our games. The boys wrestled and punched each other; the girls skipped in a line with a long rope and sometimes were allowed to join the boys for a game of kick-the-can or cuddy-loup-the-dyke. There were no holds barred because we were female. We had to take any dunts or bumps that were going.

Though we had an excess of exercise in our long walks to and from the school and in the rough-and-tumble games of the playground, the school curriculum decreed that we should have drill once a week. This was the only lesson not taken by the master himself. Instead, a fiery little man, known as the drilly, came cycling into the playground once a week and frightened the wits out of us with his sharp commands. I remember his blue uniform, his bicycle-clips, the spiky ends of his waxed moustache, and most of all his sergeant-major voice as he rapped out his orders.

'Jump to it, you idiots!'

The drilly reduced us all to jelly till we had no idea which was our right foot and which our left. We had to wheel and turn, double up, touch our toes, form into straight lines and run from one side of the playground to the other. The stragglers, or those of us who turned left instead of right, were given the full whiplash of his tongue.

We were all dolts, disgraces, and 'rubbish'; and the more he chastised us the more rubbishy we became. Many of the girls, and even some of the boys, were reduced to tears, and I longed to be brave enough to stand up to him and shout 'Shut up'! just to see what would happen. But we were all speechless with terror.

By the time the drilly cycled away in disgust with dire threats of what he would do to us next week, none of us had a scrap of confidence left. We would sooner have faced the master's tawse any day. Indeed, Auld Baldy-Heid seemed mild in comparison.

One kind word from the master meant more to us than any

amount of praise from our parents. I can still recall the thrill of pride I felt when he marked one of my essays 'Not bad.' The fact that he added 'Spelling atrocious' did not detract from my triumph. The word atrocious meant nothing to me.

Jammed together as we were, we all copied from our neighbours' jotters and helped each other with our sums, which was not always an advantage, for if one went wrong so did the lot. Similarly if we stuck when we were saying poetry there was always someone ready to prompt us in a stage-whisper which, though well-meant, often led us astray on the wrong verse.

We were always looking for diversions of any kind to break the monotony; even a mouse let loose from someone's pocket, or Bob (the braggart) firing off his water-pistol. He sat behind me and pestered the life out of me by pulling my pigtails, dipping them in his inkwell, and stuffing strange objects down the back of my neck. I used to wriggle round and swipe at him with my ruler, often, unluckily, at the moment when the teacher looked up and spotted me.

'Come out, you!' he would thunder; and what else could I do but go out and take my punishment?

We never told on each other. It was only clypes, or telltales, who did that. What would be the point? We were all in the war together. A far worse fate than getting strapped was to be told to stand out. This meant standing staring at the blank wall in a corner of the classroom in full view of everyone. There was no dunce's cap, but we felt the indignity just the same.

It was a great break when a visitor came, maybe the minister, or the laird from the Big Hoose who wandered in wearing a long cloak round his shoulders. He said a few unintelligible words to us, and once – how we loved him for it! – suggested a half-holiday which the master was forced to grant.

On one never-to-be-forgotten occasion another visitor came to the school, a strange little man who was staying with his friend, the laird, at Edgerston House. The purpose of his visit was to present prizes. For the one and only time in my life I was to be the recipient of the first prize. No wonder I was excited.

The visitor was no ordinary man. He was a famous author, so the master told us, who had written a play called *Peter Pan*. My first author and my first prize! But when he arrived I thought he looked a very odd little man in crumpled clothes and with a faraway look in his eyes. I would sooner have met Mr Anon whose works I knew better. The nearest theatre was over fifty miles away, so what chance had I of seeing *Peter Pan*?

All the same, I would have been bursting with pride if only the prize was being awarded for something to do with brains. The truth was, it was for the best-dyed egg. Even so, it would have been a triumph but for one shameful fact. I had not dyed the egg myself.

It was Jessie who had done it for me. It was she who had thought of covering the egg with a piece of lace so that it would emerge with an all-over design. It was Jessie who had put an onion in the water to give it its delicate colouring (only she called it an ingan), and it was Jessie who, by rights, ought to be receiving the prize.

I stood trembling in front of the famous man, hanging my head in shame and wondering how I could confess my sins. Sir James was very complimentary. He had never seen such a beautiful egg. If only hens could lay them like that every day, wouldn't it be wonderful? He would have a boiled egg for his breakfast every morning. What a clever little girl I was, and what pleasure he had in presenting me with the first prize which I richly deserved.

Every word he said cut me to the quick and made my sins seem more scarlet. More so when I saw the prize. It was a book of bible stories with a picture of the Good Samaritan on the cover. I clutched it under my arm and was sure that I would be struck dead.

I ran all the way home with a stitch in my side to present

the book to Jessie, its rightful owner. But she just took one look at it and said, 'Hoots, wumman, keep it. It'll lairn ye a lesson.'

And so it did; at least I determined to dye my own eggs in future.

5. Snow-siege

'I can smell snaw,' Jessie would say with a shiver, when the weather became icy cold. 'We're in for't!'

It was fun at first when the snow began to fall, great fat flakes floating from the sky like soft feathers. They settled gently on the hedges and trees, quietly piling one on top of the other till the whole farm was transformed into a dazzling white wilderness.

Sometimes the storm came on silently in the dead of night, taking us by surprise. When we woke in the morning we knew by the ominous hush that something had happened. Every sound was muffled as though the world had fallen asleep; and when we looked out of the window we could see nothing but great wreaths of snow. Everything looked fresh and new; as pure as the driven snow.

At other times it started with a blizzard. The wind wailed and howled as it blew the icy flakes horizontally against the window-panes. They froze where they landed, blotting out the light; and we knew that the storm was here to stay.

At first, while it was still possible to get out of doors, I was in my element. No going to school; every day a holiday with the snow for my plaything. Plenty of sledging and snow-balling; the thrill of seeing everything take on a sudden soft beauty. Everywhere one looked there was a lovely sight to see. Even the cart-shed became a fairy-tale castle and the tattie-bogles looked like snowmen.

There was the excitement, too, of feeling marooned. It was an adventure, like living in a story-book.

But gradually, as the farm-road became blocked and the snow relentlessly hemmed us in, I began to hate the sight of the great white wreaths that loomed over us, growing higher and wider every day. They took on monstrous shapes, like grotesque Polar beasts threatening to creep closer and swallow us up. What if we were lost for ever under a suffocating snow-blanket?

For weeks on end there was no sign of the postie, the van-man, or any human being from the outside world. No hope of even venturing outside the door. Often the hinds had to dig away the drifts before we could push it open. They made long tunnels to the steading and the byre, but it was a never-ending task, for the snow soon filled them up again. Even when it stopped falling it had frozen so hard that we were sealed in, and there was nothing for us to do but bide our time and wait for the thaw.

The worst moment came when the telephone-wires broke under the weight of snow and our last link with the outside world was gone. We could get no calls either out or in through Bella at the post office. How we longed for the shrill summons and to hear anyone, even just Bella herself, saying hullo.

The telephone was no great loss to Jessie, who hated the sight and sound of the instrument. If she was working nearby when the bell rang she gave the telephone a baleful look and ignored its summons as long as possible. At last she would snatch up the receiver and shout: 'What is't?'; then she would call out to my mother or father: 'Ye're wanted on the line,' and slam down the receiver, cutting off the call.

Even at the best of times it was not easy putting through a call. It was as well to have a comfortable seat to sit in, a book to read, or a duster in the hand to polish anything within sight, for there was often a long delay before Bella replied. Then my mother, or whoever was making the call, had to listen to the reason. Often I stood nearby and could hear her breathless voice.

'I was roond the back hingin' oot the weshin'. Ma mooth was fou' o' claes-pegs.'

Sometimes it was full of treacle-toffee. 'I was bilin' a new batch ben the hoose.'

Or: 'I was thrawin' up a scone.' Bella never baked; she threw. 'I micht thraw up a gingerbreid later on, seein' the oven's het. Are ye wantin' a number?'

Often my mother had forgotten the number because of the long delay. Or Bella would interrupt with: 'Haud on! I'll need to let the cat oot. I'll be back in a jiffy.'

The number was not so important to Bella as any news she could pass on to us or glean about what was going on upbye at the farm. How were the hens laying, had the cow calved, and when was the pig to be killed? When my mother finally got a word in edgeways and asked for a local number Bella would say, 'Och! ye needn't bother to ring them. They're oot. Awa' to Edinburgh for the day. Was't onything special?'

There were no secrets on the telephone with Bella acting as go-between; and maybe it was just as well that she knew everyone's business, for she could pass on messages from one household to another and warn us if an unexpected visitor was on his way to pay us a call.

She would ring my mother and tell her, 'That's the minister. He's been in buyin' a postal order. He's on his road up to see ye, so ye'd better pit on the kettle an' thraw up a dropscone.'

It was difficult to have any private conversations for Bella had a habit of chipping in. 'Na, na! ye're wrang! It was his wife's mother that went to Canada, no' his sister-in-law. I ken for a fact.'

And if Bella Confectionery kent for a fact, it was a fact.

No one resented these three-cornered conversations. It was understood that Bella would be listening, ready to break in with her comments. But sometimes she would bring a session to a sudden close by saying, 'Here! ye'll need to hurry up. I've got the tatties to peel.'

If a call came for us from across the Border Bella used to put on her 'fine' voice. 'Excuse me! There's a long-distance on the line. A gaintleman wishes to speak to you from New-cesstle.' She would then revert to her normal tongue and whisper, 'I think it's thon fella that sells sheep-dip. Watch him; he's an awfu' blether. Hold on, please. Ay'm putting you through.' If the man went on too long she would just cut him off in the middle of a sentence and say, 'Ay! that's enough o' him!'

All the same, Bella was our life-line, and we missed her cheerful gossip when the telephone went dead during a snow-storm. It was the most welcome sound in the world when the bell shrilled out at the end of the siege and we heard her saying, 'That's you back on the line again. Are ye a' weel? The cat's had kittlin's an' Mrs Scott's expectin'. I ken for a fact. Will ye be wantin' a number?'

While the storm lasted there were long weeks during which we heard no sound from the outside world. Wars might be raging, thrones may have fallen, friends in neighbouring farms could be lying dangerously ill. We were left in limbo knowing nothing that went on beyond the confines of the snow-bound house. Keeping ourselves alive, feeding the beasts, and trying to stay warm, were our main concerns.

There was little fear of starving, for we kept squirrel-hoards of meal and flour in the bins. There were hams hanging from the kitchen ceiling and dozens of preserved eggs laid down in vats. An entire cupboard was stocked with home-made jam: black-currant, red-currant, plum, raspberry, gooseberry, apple-jelly, and a few pots of strawberry for special occasions. But as the weeks dragged by the meals became more monotonous, and we longed for fresh food. We soon ran short of vegetables, for the turnip and potato-pits were lost under the the snow. An orange would have been a treat, or a kipper; even a baker's bun.

It was a minor tragedy if we ran short of sugar, tea, or salt, or found that our store of candles had run out. We hunted here and there for oddments and sometimes made exciting discoveries by coming across a forgotten bar of chocolate or a tin of syrup hidden in the press.

As for falling ill: 'You'd better not!' I was warned, and I did my best to oblige. Chilblains and other trivial discomforts had to be borne without a murmur. If I took a fever it just had to run its course.

The thing to do was to be as active as possible, not only to keep the circulation going but to save us from sitting about feeling sorry for ourselves. When the pipes froze and there was no running water in the house I wrapped myself up like a woollen bundle, put on my father's big boots and staggered out to collect pailfuls of snow to boil in the kettle. Every time I opened the kitchen door the bitter-cold wind nearly bowled me over and blew in a flurry of flakes which melted into rivulets on the stone flags. If Jessie was with us she was kept busy mopping up the mess with an old broom. 'Talk aboot snaw bein' clean!' she would complain. 'Ye can keep it.'

Indeed we had to keep it. As time went by I prayed every night for it to go away, but it was still there in the morning fixed more firmly than ever, as if it was there for a lifetime. How would the flowers ever grow again, and where were all the wee creepy-crawlies? There was no sign of life anywhere.

One year we lost the coal-house. It was an old shed, situated

across the road from the kitchen door, which held our store
of black diamonds, fetched by the hinds in their carts from the
depot in Jedburgh. 'Going for the coals' was a day's work for
them. Seven miles to town with their empty carts and seven
miles back with their full loads. But once they had shovelled
out the contents and stacked it up in the coal-house we felt
secure in the prospect of cosy fires for many weeks to come.

Now the snow had obliterated every trace of the shed. The
men tried to tunnel their way towards it, but they were always
off-side and never succeeded in reaching it. Luckily there were
plenty of logs and kindling in the stick-house adjoining the
kitchen. Everyone lent a hand at sawing, chopping, and carrying in the fuel to keep the fires going; but it was a never-
ending task for the great kitchen fire was like a hungry monster
greedily gobbling everything it was offered.

Though we kept as many fires going as we could it was
difficult to stay warm, in spite of 'clooty sausages' laid across
the foot of the doors to keep out the draughts and stone pigs
which we took to bed with us. Sometimes we reinforced them
with bricks heated in the oven and wrapped in flannel; but
even so we were always shivering.

Great icicles hung like stalactites from all the windows and
roofs. How we longed to see them dripping and melting, but
they grew bigger every day, and the windows were so frosted
over that we could scarcely see out. The lamps had to be lit
earlier each day, though we used fewer in order to save paraffin
and often had to feel our way about the house in the darkness.

Though I had never heard of the word claustrophobia I
knew what it meant during a long snow-siege. Everyone
seemed to be living on top of each other and it was difficult to
find sufficient outlets for high, or low spirits. Trivial quarrels
sprang up. We were all heartily sick of the sight of each other
and more particularly of the sight of the snow. It had seemed
fairylike at first, every tree a Christmas tree hanging with
glittering crystals, the whole farm softened and blurred into

beauty. But now the snow was an enemy. 'Go away! Go away!' I used to shout at it and longed for a magic wand to wave.

Trying to find the hens so that we could feed them was one of our problems. They had retired to their hen-houses at the oncome of the storm and stopped laying as if in protest. But where were the hen-houses? They were dotted all over the farm and there was no hope of reaching them. Yet somehow the Wyandottes and Minorcas and Rhode Island Reds managed to survive, emerging eventually thinner than usual and ready to peck up anything within sight.

The cattle and horses had been brought in from the hill and the fields, and shut up in their winter quarters in the sheds in the steading; and the herd had gathered as many of his flock as he could into the lambing-shed. This was a kraal-like building which Jock had built himself and roofed over with straw. Nearby was the bothy where he and the hired lambing-man had their headquarters during the lambing season.

I would have liked to live in the bothy myself away from everybody and sleep in the truckle-bed with its straw palliasse. There was an open fire where the herd heated milk for the lambs and sometimes fried ham or cooked porridge for himself. The bothy had a thatched roof, a small window like a watching eye, and a story-book air about it as if Wee Willie Winkle might live there.

On days when we were not snow-bound I sometimes went there and sat with Jock while he made a new crook, watching every move as he patiently planed the wood and polished the head.

'I'd never get by withoot a crook,' he used to tell me. 'Man-lassie! it's like ma third hand.'

True enough, Jock used his crooks in a dozen different ways: to lever himself over a dyke, to cleek a lamb round the neck (sometimes to cleek me, too, if I fell into a ditch), to poke down into the snow in search of buried sheep, to dowse the lambs at dipping-time. It was not only a third, but a fourth hand to him.

I was convinced that Jock was the cleverest man in the world. The things he knew! Often I watched him coaxing a ewe to take on a motherless lamb after her own had died. Sometimes she butted the lamb out of the way – and butted the herd, too – but he did not give in. He went quietly away, skinned off the complete covering from the dead lamb and slung it over the orphan's back. This time when he carried the motherless bairn and set it down beside the ewe, she did not reject it. She sniffed at it, recognising the smell of her own lamb, and before long it was snuggling against her, sucking contentedly.

It was hard going for the herd during a storm. He had literally to fight his way through the snow to save as many of his flock as possible. Sometimes he had to dig them out of the drifts, and it amazed me to find how they could keep alive for days, even weeks, in such conditions and without any food. Sheep, it seemed, were not as silly as they looked. Certainly they had enough sense to preserve themselves.

Sometimes Jock came into the kitchen to fetch more milk and stood in the lamplight with the snow dripping off him and little icicles hanging from his eyebrows. The collies would lie down beside me on the rug, put their heads on their paws, and instantly fall asleep.

It was not often that Jessie spoke to her brother, but sometimes she would say: 'Sit doon, man, an' drink a cup o' tea.' But Jock never did. Maybe he would drink the tea, but he would not sit down.

'It I sit, I'll stert gantin',' he declared, 'an' fa' asleep, like the dogs.' Poor things! their dreams were short. 'Up, Jed! Come on, Jess! Ootbye!' And away they went into the cold, leaving pools of water on the floor where the snow had melted. Exhausted or not, they never disobeyed their master's commands.

It was difficult to remember which day of the week it was. Indeed, it mattered little; they were all the same. Too much the same. The one thing we were all waiting for was the thaw.

The men tried to open a pathway down the road by digging their way through the drifts, but it was a Herculanean task. Then at last they succeeded in dragging out the old snow-plough from the cart-shed and yoking in the Clydesdales.

They made many false starts. The horses floundered up to their bellies in the snow, slipping and sliding on the icy surface. Sometimes they could only struggle on for a few yards before they came to a standstill and the men were forced to unyoke them again.

Day after day they tried, making a little more progress each time till at length – oh! happy day – they got as far as the cottages and disappeared from sight.

Their object was to reach the farm road-end in the hope that the main road had been opened up by the big County Council snow-plough and they might catch the vanman or even get as far as Bella's shop for supplies.

By now the larder was growing emptier. We had eaten our way through the hams, and had a surfeit of barley scones and porridge. My mother concocted various soups and puddings as best she could, but we hankered after variety. What I longed for most were some sweets or even a stick of sugar-ally.

We watched and waited eagerly for the men's return. They had taken huge sacks with them to contain any scran they could forage, and it was a crushing disappointment if they came back empty-handed and exhausted, shaking their heads to let us know their mission had failed. But they would try again tomorrow.

When at last they succeeded it was better than Christmas. The men were all smiles as they lugged in the bulging sacks and hoisted them on to the kitchen table while we gathered round, eagerly watching to see what would emerge. Loaves of bread, sausages, newspapers, letters, tobacco, sweets, candles, matches, tea, sugar. Every single item was welcome.

Most welcome of all was any scrap of local news the men had managed to glean. Fancy! they had met not only Bella Confectionery, but Mary-Anne, Wat-the-Baker, the gamey, and the postie. Such richness! They had heard that the Carter Bar was still blocked, that the Scotts, like us, were snow-bound, that the minister was down with 'flu, that some ruler in a foreign country had been deposed; but that did not interest us as much as the greatest news of all. The thaw was on its way.

What a difference the prospect of freedom made to our spirits! A weight seemed to be lifted off us and we began to laugh and sing and talk about all the things we would do when we were released. Imagine riding once more in the gig with Flora trotting along the open road! Even the thought of going back to school filled me with elation.

This feeling of euphoria did not last. Strangely enough, it was the last lap that was the worst. Tempers that were frayed before became even more ragged as the reaction set in, and we seemed to be even more on top of each other.

Every day we waited impatiently for the promised thaw but it seemed reluctant to come. When it did it was even more uncomfortable than the storm. Nothing on earth can be colder and more miserable than a 'cold thaw', with everything looking bleak and the snow drip-drip-dripping as it slowly melts away.

Jessie had to hound me out of the house. 'Awa' ootbye an' get some colour into your cheeks. Ye're a peelly-wally object.'

Though I had been gasping for fresh air, the discomfort of slopping about in the slush was so great that I clung, shivering, to the fireside. The snow began to look old and dirty. Soon it ran like rivers, oozing under the kitchen door, into the hall, and all over the place. Water seemed to cascade everywhere, from burst pipes, from melting icicles, from rooftops when the snow came thudding down like an avalanche.

I had to be careful not to get buried under it for it could have felled me to the ground. There were times when I longed for it to freeze again so that everything could be neat and clean. But gradually I could see patches of black earth and sense the first faint signs of spring. The cocks and hens emerged from the hen-houses to begin their clucking and pecking, and soon the whole farm stirred to life once more.

Looking back, I wonder how we survived the long spell indoors without the diversion of television or radio. But we had a great compensation in what Jessie called the 'grammy-phone'.

It was a friendly old machine with an immense fluted horn. I used to stick my head inside it trying to get closer to Melba or Caruso. Sometimes I stuffed my doll in there, too, or used the horn as a secret hiding-place for other treasures. My elders could always tell from the muffled sounds if that bairn had been at it again.

The records had been played so often that I knew every tune inside-out and was word-perfect with every song. Not that there were many, and few of them without a flaw. Most of them were scarred and scratched but I knew the exact spot at which the needle would stick and sat on the table beside the machine ready to pick up the arm and lift it over the obstacle. Otherwise there would be a dreadful din when Harry Lauder repeated himself over and over in the midst of 'Stop Your Ticklin', Jock' till even the cat went and hid under the table.

I liked a good-going band with a rousing tune and would often replay the best bits, shifting the needle back to the cheery place. Playing the gramophone was anything but a passive performance. It entailed a great deal of hard labour but it was worth the effort. To me it was a magic music-box.

First, the unwieldy object had to be lifted on to the table, a task far beyond my capacity. I always had to badger a grown-

up into lending a helping hand. Sometimes Jessie obliged but
not without a protest.

'Can ye no' let's have some peace an' quiet?'

All the same she was not averse to music while she worked
and even joined in now and again when 'the man on the
grammyphone' was singing a song.

When it was safely set on the table I hunted through the
small pile of records till I found a favourite, then set it on the
turn-table and inserted a new needle if I could find one in the
wee tin box with a picture of a dog on the lid, but usually they
were old and rusty. Sometimes I had to recall Jessie to help with
the cranking of the handle and often the record would run
down half-way through with a disembodied voice groaning
to a standstill.

It was fun to have such power over the musicians. I could
stop them and start them, I could make them go faster or
slower. Poor things! they were sadly overworked. Little
wonder their voices sounded so wheezy as if they had sung
themselves hoarse, for I gave them little rest and could never
get over the wonder of watching the records spinning round
and round.

Even before I could read the names on the labels I could tell
by the scratches on the surface which was 'The Skye Boat Song'
or 'The Blue Danube'. Later on in life I was surprised to hear
a record playing all the way through without ever sticking.
Even now when I hear an orchestra performing one of the
familiar pieces I wait for the musicians to falter at the scratchy
bit, and am faintly disappointed when they sail on without
having to be helped over the hurdle.

I had not my father's facility but I tried to make music myself, of a kind, on the old upright piano in the parlour-drawing-
room. It was a miracle that it remained upright considering
the amount of punishment it had to take and the fact that it
had to be thumped so hard to get any sound out of it at all. I
liked its honky-tonk tinkle when the yellowed keys were

struck, though there were some that remained silent no matter how hard they were hit.

Later on it was replaced by the good piano, a shining instrument with a fine tone and without a scratch on it. But I liked the old one best with its pink satin front and its ornate candlesticks which could be swung from the side. It had character if nothing else. Sometimes I twirled round and round on the piano-stool before dizzily trying to vamp out 'The Rosebud Waltz' or 'Come O'er the Stream, Charlie.'

When the spirit moved her, Miss Todd, the music teacher, came cycling up the bumpy farm-road on her wobbly bicycle to give me a lesson of sorts. If I saw her in time I ran away and hid up a tree or under the reaper in the cart-shed. But sometimes I was discovered and dragged, protesting, into her presence where I had to submit to being put through my paces with *Hemy's Tutor for the Pianoforte* propped up in front of me.

Sitting in the rocking-chair drinking tea and eating homemade cake, she would say, 'Right, dear, we'll start with the scales.'

I was fed up with scales but I played them as softly as I could so that the wrong notes would sound less jarring. Soon, if I was lucky, I would hear the tea-cup being laid down and a gentle snore coming from the direction of the rocking-chair. I could prop up *Little Women* in place of the hated *Tutor* and let my fingers stray where they pleased while I had a good read.

If she was in a wideawake mood I would be forced to go through the whole rickmatick from crotchets to semi-quavers ending with 'The Bluebells of Scotland' (two-four time, count four quavers in a bar). With variations.

I could never see the point of variations. Having played the thing in one way why go through the torture of adding twiddly-bits just to make it different? It was difficult enough to keep two hands going at the one time. My left, alas! seldom knew what my right was doing.

I thumped my way through 'Le Carnival de Venise' and 'Rousseau's Dream', which must have sounded more like a nightmare to poor Miss Todd; but 'The Harmonious Blacksmith' was the greatest misnomer of the lot. I much preferred making up my own tunes and not bothering about semibreves. They were all varied versions, but improved, I thought, of 'Scots Wha Hae' or 'Pop Goes the Weasel'.

'You're getting on, dear,' lied Miss Todd, putting on her hat, 'but you'll need to stick in. Remember those scales.'

'Oh yes, I will,' I promised, and forgot both Miss Todd and the scales the moment she went wobbling away down the road on her bicycle.

Now and then a seedy-looking gent, almost as ancient as the piano itself, came out from the town to tune it. He shuffled into the room with his tuning-fork in his hand, shook his head when he saw the piano and said, 'Past hope!'

All the same he had a kind of love-hate for the old instrument and was as proud as punch when he had patched it up and unstuck the keys. He always sat down when he was finished to try it out, playing a flamboyant piece all arpeggios and crossed hands. I thought him better than Paderewski on the gramophone and wondered why *he* had not made a record.

It was fun to watch how he took the piano to pieces. Off came the back, sides, and front. Then he turned up his nose and sent me scurrying for dusters. No wonder, considering the amount of fluff inside, and not only fluff. Goodness knows how so many extraneous objects found their way into the inner recesses, but they did.

Once the tuner came across a family of mice nesting in a corner and we had a high old time chasing them out of the house before the kitchen cat could get at them. There was no doubt that 'The Bluebells of Scotland' sounded better without them.

The old piano was kept busy when visitors came to spend the night. It was an understood thing that they would all help to entertain each other. Everyone was prepared to do a turn and indeed would have been offended if not asked to perform.

I kept well out of sight, usually under the sofa, in case I was called on to do my piece, but the visitors showed no signs of reluctance. The trouble often was to get them to stop.

There was not much variety in their repertoire. I knew for certain that the minister would start with 'When We Go Down the Vale, Lad' sung in a very low key especially if the piano-tuner had not visited us lately. He kept his eyes closed while he sang and swayed from side to side as if he was in a trance. His encore was invariably 'Juanita' which he rendered so soulfully that it brought tears to his own eyes, closed or not.

It was a relief to be cheered up by my father with one of his comic songs. 'When Father Papered the Parlour' and 'Paddy McGinty's Goat' were my favourites. Sometimes he sang 'The Galloping Major' using an old kitchen chair as his charger.

My mother played the accompaniments and she, too, sometimes sang a solo, though her songs were all tear-jerkers. I remember a touching little ditty called, believe it or not, 'Close the Shutters, Willy's Dead' which made me crawl further under the sofa. Another had an even more pathetic refrain: 'Turn your face to the wall, Daddy, Mother's no longer here.' It brought a lump to my throat every time I heard it.

Luckily it was not long before someone tuned up the fiddle and the cheerful strains of 'My Love She's but a Lassie Yet' helped to banish my gloom. And often the evening ended in a kitchen dance in which I could join if I had not been chased off to bed. The table was pushed to the side, the hearthrug rolled back and the cats and dogs shooed out of the way.

Sometimes I just sat in a corner watching and pretending I was not there, but on occasions I was brought in to make up a set if they ran short of someone for the Circassian Circle or the Eightsome Reel. Sometimes I was invited to dance a polka and had difficulty in keeping my feet out of the way of my partner's boots as he hopped like a carthorse round the kitchen.

It was strange to watch the grown-ups enjoying themselves with such abandon. The dances were like games and the dancers like children. They swung each other off their feet at the Lancers and went chasing up and down the middle at Drops o' Brandy. Their cheeks grew flushed and their eyes bright. Imagine the minister, so pompous in the pulpit, discarding his jacket and shouting 'Hooch!' like an overgrown schoolboy! And staid Mrs Scott kilting up her skirts and showing her garters. Black elastic.

It somehow gave me hope to realize that fun was not finished when folk grew old. Old! Doubtless some of the company had not yet reached their thirties. Normally their conversation was as dull as ditch-water. Crops, the price of lambs, recipes, the government, and endless talk about the weather. Never ideas-talk or fantasy-talk, the kind I liked best. 'Imagine what it would be like to have wings.' Or, 'What would you do with three magic wishes?' Grown-ups were too realistic to indulge in such foolish bairn-talk.

Usually, that is! Now they were chattering like children digging each other in the ribs and laughing till the tears ran down their cheeks. My own eyes grew heavy with sleep and I was hustled off to bed with the strains of fiddle-music growing fainter in my ears.

The sad thing was, it did not last. Next morning my elders had reverted to normal, going about their dull duties with set lips, looking a little tired and crosser than usual. If I tried to cheer them up by playing 'Polly-Wolly-Doodle' on the gramophone they would say sharply, 'Shut off that noise!' What had been fun and frolic the night before was now frowned upon. I would never, I thought, be able to understand old folk, never!

I liked to hear the bothy-ballads which the hinds sometimes sang in the stable while they were grooming their horses. Cornkisters they were called. Farmworkers used to sit on the old corn-'kists', dunting their feet against the wooden sides to beat out an accompaniment to their songs. They were rumbustious, rollicking songs with a story in them which went on for verse after verse, all about kitchie-lasses, tattie-howking and 'The Muckin' o' Geordie's Byre.' The choruses were full of fol-d-rols and tooral-oorals, in which anyone could join, even the horses jangling their harness.

The best musical sounds could be heard in the open air from the whaups, the blackies, and the shilfies. I liked to listen to the cuckoo calling 'at once far off and near'. Sometimes I lay in the long grass in the cow-gang watching a skylark hovering overhead, singing its heart out. What was it trying to say? 'Aren't we lucky to be alive?'

My most vivid musical memory is of my brother practising the fiddle after I had gone to bed. He was persistent if nothing else. I used to stuff my head under the pillow to muffle the screeches of catgut as he went over the same piece again and again, going back to pick up the wrong notes like dropped stitches.

It was the beginning, I feel sure, of my lifelong insomnia. Or maybe my sleeplessness started with that frightening prayer I was forced to say before going to bed every night.

> Now I lay me down to sleep,
> I pray the Lord my soul to keep.
> If I should die before I wake
> I pray the Lord my soul to take.

I once asked Jessie if the Lord really would take my soul.

'Ay, nae doot!' she said, firmly tucking me in, 'if ye dinna gang to sleep quick.'

But how could I go to sleep quick with 'Handel's Largo', slightly off-key, resounding in my ears?

6. Queen of the Castle

Even when I was a toddler I felt, as I do now, the urgent need to retire into my shell, to have long silences, to watch people, maybe, from a distance but not to speak to them, to think my own thoughts, above all not to do what *They* want.

It is a form of self-indulgence that was easy enough to put into practice on the farm. I just walked out of the door, ignored all enquiries as to where I was going and made my way up to the hill.

There I took up temporary residence in the ruined Border keep, with no one to disturb me except the whaups, a rabbit bolting out of the bracken, or a sheep wandering in to crop the grass on the castle floor.

The grim grey fortress was not a cosy place in which to play houses especially if the wind was howling round the draughty pile, but at least it was far enough away from *Them*. I could ignore the clanging of the dinner-bell, which I could only hear anyway if the wind was in the right direction, tolled from the farmhouse for the purpose of bringing me to heel.

I scaled the crumbling walls dislodging another old stone here and there and sat looking out across no-man's-land to the Border. Roxburghshire on my side, Northumberland on the other where the enemy used to gather their forces to invade us and where my friend Kate now lived.

Everything was peaceful. No warlike cries, no clash of weapons, no furtive figures creeping across the frontier. Only the postie on his bicycle or the baker with his horse-and-cart. All the same I kept a catapult ready just in case. *Wha daur meddle wi' me?*

Here I was queen. No one could order me about. A couple of crows had built untidy nests in one of the crannies but I did not mind them squatting in my keep. It was human beings I wanted to avoid. Jock-the-herd was the only visitor I ever made welcome.

Household chores in the castle were easily done. They consisted of picking up tumbled stones from the floor and tidying away fallen leaves. No rubbing and scrubbing, no polishing and dusting. This was a far more sensible way of living than within the confines of a house which ate up time and energy with its constant demands for cleanliness. Who needed ornaments? The Cheviot hills were a better sight than a mantelpiece full of china whigmaleeries.

When I was hungry I ate raw turnips, crab-apples or any berries I could find. Sugar-ally was my favourite beverage when I could get it. A liquorice-stick shaken up in a lemonade-bottle filled with water from the burn. It never slaked my thirst but it had a nice tangy taste and left me with a blue-black moustache.

'Man-lassie! ye'll puzzen yoursel',' the herd warned me when he wandered into my precincts, but he was not averse to taking a swig himself, wiping away the froth from his face with the back of his hand.

Jock warned me, too, if the bull was on the hill and likely to roam in my direction.

'Watch oot! He's no' to be trusted, the ugly brute!'

True, the bull was no beauty with a ring through his nose and a vicious glint in his eye, but I thought it a pity that nobody had a kind word for him. Poor thing, he was just a beast. Maybe he only wanted to play.

I changed my mind one day when I had ignored the herd's warning and the 'ugly brute' came charging at me. I was gathering an armful of dried bracken and branches of whinbushes in the hope of lighting a blaze in the great fireplace big enough to roast an ox.

When I heard the bull bellowing behind me I dropped my bundle, took to my heels and scaled up the castle wall at the double. I had to sit there for hours, marooned, while the bull pawed the ground and roared up at me. Perhaps he was only making friendly noises. 'Come down and play.' But I felt it safer to stay where I was till Jock and his dogs came to rescue me.

'Man-lassie! I tell't ye. Wull ye never lairn?'

It was disheartening to find how often grown-ups were right and how they relished pointing out my mistakes. 'See how clever we are,' they seemed to be saying. 'We know best. We never do anything wrong.' How much better I would have liked them if they did!

The most unwelcome guests who came prowling round my castle were the archaeologists. The diggers, I called them. They were an earnest group of men and women who came from goodness-knows-where, carrying picks, shovels, spades, and little hammers.

I had no idea what they were looking for but whatever it was they never found me. I hid up the great chimney and stayed there as still as a statue while they poked around the place as if it belonged to them. Sometimes they gathered in an excited huddle and I concluded they must have unearthed some ancient relic. More often it was only a biscuit-tin or one of my discarded sugar-ally bottles.

I had a hidden hoard myself but I was not going to let on to the diggers. In the course of my residence in the keep I had discovered many old bones, stones, weapons, and cooking-utensils which I kept in a hidey-hole up on the look-out tower near one of the crow's nests. It was my own private museum. For all I know it is there to this day.

I hated when the hunt came galloping across the hillside in full cry giving chase to a frightened fox, though it was a splendid sight. It was exciting to hear the huntsman's horn and to see the pink coats, but the blood-curdling baying of the dogs filled my heart with horror. If the huntsman had lost the trail and stopped to ask me the way I would have pointed in the wrong direction, though the hounds would not have been so easily foiled.

'Blood!' they seemed to be saying. 'We want blood!' With their noses to the ground they could pick up the scent and ruthlessly follow their prey to the end, though, thank goodness, I was never in at the kill. We had a fox head hanging on the wall near the front door. He seemed to grin down on everyone who came in, smiling even in death.

It was wonderful playing houses in the keep when the weather was sunny. Not so pleasant if a sudden storm sprang up. I had an old waterproof sheet under which I could shelter from the rain, for the roof – what was left of it – leaked so badly that it was almost wetter inside than out.

When the wind howled round the crumbling ruin there was an added danger. Sometimes a rattle of loose stones blew down on my head and I had to dodge out of the way to avoid being hit, not that I always succeeded, and had plenty of bumps and bruises to show for it but it was all part of the fun.

What must it have been like, I wondered, in the days when the keep was occupied as a fortress? I tried to picture it with its roof on and great logs crackling up the chimney, with always someone watching from the look-out tower? Would there be children there, like me, playing houses?

Near at hand there was a purling burn, the small Jed, where I sometimes went to wade when the weather was hot. I had to slither down a craggy bank to reach it, past a mysterious cave where the reivers used to hide their loot in bygone days. I seldom ventured in for it was full of eerie rustles. A badger might came darting out of the darkness or a large bird fly in my face. Creepy-crawlies of all descriptions made their homes there, and there was no knowing who else. A bogle maybe or a strange monster with two heads.

The Jed was a fascinating winding burn, like the one in J. B. Selkirk's poem.

> Ah, Tam! gie me a Border burn
> That canna rin withoot a turn,
> An' wi' its bonnie babble fills
> The glens amang oor native hills.
> How men that ance have kent aboot it
> Can live their efter-lives withoot it
> I canna tell, for day an' nicht
> It comes unca'd-for to my sicht.

True enough, it is the river Jed that I can see with my inward eye, especially on sleepless nights when my mind roams back over half-forgotten childhood scenes.

In every season of the year there was something different to see on its banks. In spring and summer a profusion of ferns and wildflowers grew there: bluebells, primroses, marsh-marigolds like little yellow butter-balls, and sturdy reeds which I pulled up and plaited into pigtails after eating the juiciest parts of the stems. If I hunted long enough I could find small wild strawberries which tasted sharp and delicious.

In autumn the russet-red and golden leaves of the old trees, relics of the original Jedforest, made a splash of brilliant colour against the sky. Later, when they blew off and lay like a thick carpet, I liked to rustle through them almost up to the knees in bright leaves. Even in winter the bare branches looked elegant, stretching graceful arms from their gnarled trunks. There was always something worth looking at, at any time.

Colourful birds, too, to be seen at the waterside. Kingfishers with brilliant plumage skimming down from the sky, water-wagtails hopping from stone to stone, a long-legged heron standing pensively in midstream. They all seemed to live intense self-contained lives, not grouping together like humans but pursuing their own private ploys. I wondered if the different species could understand each other's language and if they ever greeted each other in passing.

In stormy weather the water came tumbling down from the hills in a hurry, drowning the buttercups on the bank and carrying some strange objects before it. Sometimes an old bedstead came floating by or a dead sheep. Tin cans, empty bottles, broken umbrellas, straw hats, bicycle-tyres and old boots all came whirling by as if playing follow-my-leader. Some of them stuck going round the bend and I could either rescue them if they were worth retrieving or give them a push to send them on their way. It reminded me of a song my father used to sing.

> The burn was big wi' spate,
> An' there cam' tummlin' doon
> Tapsulteerie the half o' a gate,
> An auld fish hake, an' a great muckle skate,
> An' a lum hat wantin' the croon.

Now and then I found something useful: an old tennis-ball, a mouth-organ, a tin soldier, or a cracked teapot which came in handy when playing houses. I was always hopeful that I might find real treasure, perhaps a ruby ring, but the nearest I came to it was when I fished out a sliver bracelet and found it was made of wire.

There were two ways of getting across the Jed. Three in

winter when the river was frozen and one could just walk across the ice. One was by stepping-stone, but the stones were so unsteady and set at such awkward angles that I often over-balanced and tumbled into the water.

The other was even more adventurous and had that spark of danger that appealed to me so that I had to goad myself on before I dared attempt it. At one point a decrepit wooden gate hung across the water. The water-gate, we called it. It had been put there to prevent cattle from wandering down the river, and was suspended from a stout spar, like a great log of wood. The thing to do was to climb up on top of the gate and sidle across while clinging hand-over-hand to the overhead spar.

The old gate made creaking noises and swayed backwards and forwards at each of my sideways steps. Often I got stuck in the middle too terrified to make another move especially if the burn was in spate. I had to hound myself on inch by inch till I reached the other side.

This was theoretically a short-cut to the little village of Camptown, though in reality it would have been quicker to go round by the road, though not half the adventure. Once across, I could scramble up another steep bank and arrive, breathless and bedraggled, at the back of my granny's house. I would visit her, do some odd jobs, have a dip into the sweet-tin, and, if I had been sent on a message, go to Bella Confectionery's to make my purchases.

The return journey was the most difficult if I had two or three packages to carry. Perhaps sugar, salt, or tea. The trick was to toss them one by one across the Jed at its narrowest point, always hoping the bags would not burst, before attempt-ing to cross myself. Alas! a bag often did burst, and once a tin of mustard fell short and went floating away, like the lum hat, in the company of a bottomless pail and an old Wellington boot.

I would get what-for when I reached home, but this time

I knew I would deserve it. I did not always understand the
reasons why grown-ups meted out punishment, though I was
always aware of the power they had to rule my life, and longed
for the day when I could make my own decisions.

Often I sensed that their psychology was wrong. Why, for
instance, could they not just let me sit still and think, if I wanted
to, instead of rousing me out of my reverie. 'Come on! Don't
sit mumping there. Can't you go and *do* something?'

Even at an early age children need to withdraw within
themselves without constantly being harassed with questions.
'What are you doing? Where have you been? Why are you
sitting still?'

It seems difficult when one is young to please one's elders.
Either we are too noisy or too quiet. What are we to do?
Perhaps this is when we first start learning to deceive, to put
on masks and become not ourselves but what our elders expect
us to be: perfect replicas of our fathers or mothers.

I was lucky in that my parents had others to think about and
I could often escape their notice. I was good at the game, pretending not to hear, or vanishing from sight when I thought
they were about to pounce on me.

Above all, I could retreat to my crumbling castle. Then
suddenly I would have enough of the long loneliness. When
the sun began to fade and strange shadows crept across the
hillside I would shiver and think of the pleasures of human
companionship. All that I had tried to avoid before. I felt a
sense of emptiness, more than mere hunger, and ran away from
the keep with never a backward glance, straining my eyes for a
sight of the lamplight shining from the kitchen window.

Maybe I would get a slap from Jessie when I went in but
I would even enjoy that. There would be a dinner-y smell
from the pots and pans on the fire and all the noise and bustle
of the household going on around me. I would no longer be a
lone bairn but part of a family.

This, at that moment, was what I wanted most.

How can we hope to recapture that magic moment, the split-second almost, when we made the greatest discovery of our young lives?

We could read!

It came to me like a bolt from the blue. One moment I was painfully trying with prodding finger to decipher the a's and b's in my lesson-book. The next moment the revelation happened. I could form the letters into words.

They were inane enough words. 'The cat is fat. The dog can run. The cow says "Moo".' But at least I was reading. The door was opened wide; where might it lead to?

Having learned a new skill I could never get enough of it. From then on I became, and have remained, an obsessive gobbler-up of books. The sight of printed words, of hand-writing even, had always fascinated me as a child. Now that I could make some sense out of the symbols I wanted to rush forward and devour everything that had ever been written. Never mind the long words. I could skip over them and still get some of the meaning. Even the staid *Scotsman* was fodder for me. If I could find nothing better I would try to read the Fat-Stock Prices or the Births, Marriages and Deaths. Anything as long as it was words.

I soon tired of Henny-Penny and the insipid creatures in the school reading-book. We seldom had new ones. To save expense school books were handed down like old clothes from one member of the family to another, till they became tattier and tattier, with torn pages and everyone's scribbles in the margins.

The stories in the reading-book were far too feeble to satisfy my thirst. I wanted real books with real stories, but alas! there was no school library. How I envy the school-children of today with their bright classrooms and the wealth of books at their command. A new one to read every day of their lives, if they like!

At the village school there was only one shelf which contained the entire library, such as it was. Ten dusty volumes of *Tales of the Borders*. To the master's sarcastic amusement I borrowed them one by one and galloped through them, not really understanding the contents. They were all much of a muchness. Bloodthirsty tales of dreadful deeds at dead of night, of headless horsemen, dismembered bodies, and ghostly warriors. They gave me little more than mental indigestion, but at least I learned some new words if not how to pronounce them. Fidelity, for instance, which for long enough I thought of as fiddle-ty.

There were books at home but not enough. I raced through everything in the bookcase, understanding little of *A Journey to the Amazon* and less of *The Life of Wellington*. I read my brother's *Robin Hood*, my sister's *School Friend* and my own *Chatterbox* over and over again. Re-reading was, and still is, one of my favourite occupations like getting to know an old friend even better. Sometimes I would read a book right through to the end and then start straight off again at the beginning, always finding something new that I had missed before.

The few children's books in the house, belonging to a previous generation, were all very sad and holy, with titles like *Jessica's First Prayer*. I often wished I could find one about a bad child like myself, but the heroines were all too good to live and, indeed, most of them died young.

Reading and guilt were mixed up in my mind. I still have the feeling that a grown-up will come along and snatch the book out of my hand. Jessie, particularly, made me feel I was committing a crime.

'Tak' your heid oot that book an' do something useful,' she would say.

Reading was bad for the eyes, bad for the health, bad for the mind. 'Filling your head with nonsense,' according to my elders. Especially when they discovered me reading the servant-lasses' novelettes: cheap paper-covered trash with pictures – innocent enough – on the outside. I did not think much of them myself, they were just something to read, but they had too much love in them. I was all for handsome princes marrying beautiful princesses, but the novelettes were on a lower level with too much sloppy talk in them.

Doing something useful meant knitting or sewing. I was never any good at hemming and back-stitching. The only garment I ever finished was a camisole that would have fitted a giantess, dotted with drops of blood from my fingers. Knitting was more to my liking, especially when I could combine it with reading. I soon learned the trick of plaining and purling with a book propped up on the arm of an easy-chair. In that way I could continue to fill my head with nonsense while satisfying the grown-ups that I was not wasting my time. *The Wide Wide World* and turning the heel of a sock always go together in my mind.

I dropped the odd tear along with the odd stitch for I liked reading hardship stories – as I believe most young people do – where the emotions of fear or pity could be stretched to the full. *The Little Match-Girl* always brought a lump to my throat though I knew it was only a story. Later, I wallowed in *Hard Times*, longing to help Dickens' characters over their difficulties (though somehow I could never swallow Little Nell), and if I could have re-written the books, I would have given everyone a happy ending.

What power the writers had! They could kill off a character at the stroke of a pen, or cure someone lying sick of a dangerous illness. They could carry the reader over the seas – even under the water, in the case of Jules Verne – and make him laugh or cry. I began to long for the same power; not only to read books but to write them.

There was no planned reading for me in my young days. Every Christmas I was given an Annual, take it or leave it. The school stories were remote from anything I had experienced, with their dormitories, tuck-boxes, hockey-matches, and gym-tunics. None of the characters seemed to come to life or to speak like a real human being.

I preferred the stories in the Bible. I could believe in Daniel in the Lions' Den and Joseph and his Brethren; but even at an early age I puzzled about Jesus. Where had he been during all the missing years? Why had he not begun his ministry earlier and had more time on earth to teach and heal? The Bible bewildered me in many ways, yet it was a fascinating book to read no matter how bamboozled I was by its strange language.

Nothing could surpass the thrill of opening a new book I had not read before. This happened on rare occasions, mainly when there was a sale somewhere in the district. A roup. My parents were faithful attenders of such affairs, where farm-implements and household goods were being sold off, and invariably bought something to bring home: a kitchen chair, a picture, a clock, or a jelly-pan. Better still, a bundle of books. 'Miscellaneous volumes: one-and-sixpence.'

Sometimes they had to be purchased in a lot, along with cracked ornaments, an old kettle, even a wooden cradle; and if they had been nuggets of pure gold I would not have welcomed them half as eagerly.

Black Beauty came out of the cradle and so did *Easy Geometry*, which I thought was a very dry read and not a bit easy at all, but I had to take the good with the bad. Often, alas! I was left high and dry in the middle of a sentence when I discovered that pages were missing. I was full grown before I knew that Robinson Crusoe had been rescued from the desert island, and Oliver Twist's early life was a mystery to me for years.

From reading to writing was the next natural step though spelling was still a hurdle. At school the master had a passion for parsing which took all the fun out of reading and could kill a sentence stone dead. But at least he started us off on 'imaginative writing' though his own imagination fell flat when it came to inventing subjects for our essays. If only he had let us choose our own! His were deadly dull.

'Scotland's Heritage' – whatever that meant – was one of his stand-bys; and 'A Day at the Seaside', which was also beyond our ken since none of us had ever been there. Or, 'My Favourite Hobby'.

We all chewed despairingly at our pencils and keeked at each other's jotters to see if there was anything worth copying. One shepherd-boy, after pondering over the subject for ages, wrote laboriously, 'I have not got a hoby.' End of essay!

I set down my thoughts as well as I could, making up hobbies for the sake of filling a few lines. They were so improbable that Auld Badly-Heid glowered at me after reading my efforts and barked out, 'Rubbish!' Collecting skeletons, converting salt into gold by means of magic, and flying round the world on invisible wings were hardly hobbies he could swallow.

'Rubbish!' he kept repeating. But sometimes – a fate worse than death – he would call me out and make me stand up in front of the class to read out the rubbish, with everyone sniggering at me and the boys making me their target for inky pellets. I was never sure whether the master meant it as a compliment to me or an Awful Warning to the rest of the pupils, but I considered it nothing more than a penance.

At that period in my life I had two fixed ambitions. One was to keep a sweet-shop, like Bella Confectionery's, without any customers. What bliss it would be to help myself from every bottle and jar, to weigh out caramels and fill three-cornered pokes with toffee, knowing that I could eat my way through the lot without paying for them.

The other was to be let loose to browse in an enormous room filled from floor to ceiling with books, without anyone there to tell me to go and do something useful. Perhaps I was visualizing a place I had never yet seen but where in later years I would spend many a happy hour. A public library. Even today I tremble with excitement every time I enter the portals of one of these book-palaces. And, going into anyone's house, I never notice the carpets or the furnishings. Only the contents of the bookcases.

We had, of course, a real author in the Borders. Sir Walter Scott. But he was dead long ago.

'Ay! he was a great man, Wattie,' the master used to tell us, as if he had known him personally. Rabbie, too, had been a grand fellow, though some of his poetry was best not repeated. It was safer to stick to Anon, who was purer.

The great revelation of reading meant so much to me that I wanted to pass it on to everyone else, as if I alone had made the magical discovery. I even tried to smit Jock-the-herd with my enthusiasm.

'Do you never read?' I asked him one day when he was leaning against a dyke staring at the sheep and preparing to smoke his pipe. This was no straightforward operation. The pipe had to be scraped out first with a knife, then the herd took a tin box from his pocket and began the careful process of filling the bowl, pressing down the tobacco with his thumb, before starting another search through his pockets for a box of matches. It took two or three attempts, more on a windy day, before the tobacco began to glow. Once it was going to his satisfaction Jock covered the bowl with a small metal lid with air-holes in it, and at last the deed was done.

'Read!' he said, puffing out a great gust of smoke. 'I tak' a look at the papers noo an' then.'

'But would you not like to read a book?' I persisted. The papers had nothing in them but bad news and politics.

'A book? Man-lassie, what wad I want wi' a book?

I tried to tempt him with *What Katy Did* but he was not on for it. 'If it had something to dae wi' sheep-dip, I micht gie it a try. But I'm no' fond o' stories.'

Jessie on the other hand liked what she called a good book. A sentimental story with a happy ending. Especially one written by Annie S. Swan who supplied wholesome serials for the *People's Friend*. But Jessie would only indulge in reading after she had completed every useful task. If she had finished the darning and mending she would pick up her story and settle down to read a few pages, tut-tutting now and again if she disapproved of any of the characters.

Sometimes she discussed the stories with me, as if all the people in them were alive.

'Fancy Mary Graham no' seein' through thon chap! I never liked the soond o' him frae the beginnin.' I kent he was efter her siller. She'll be better-aff in the hinner-end wi' her cousin John. Though, mind ye, I'm no' keen on cousins gettin' mairret. . . .'

Jessie would listen to me, too, often at milking-time while I gave her a precis of what I was reading. I remember giving her chapter and verse about *Uncle Tom's Cabin* and trying to arouse her compassion over the injusticies to the poor slaves. Neither of us had ever seen a coloured person in our lives. 'Though I've a guid idea,' Jessie told me, 'for I ance saw the Darkey-Troupe, but they were only blackened for the nicht.'

I often wondered how words got on to the printed page. I knew they had originally come out of someone's head, Annie S. Swan's or Mr Charles Dickens', but that was as far as I could visualize the process. In my own writings I copied the style of whatever book I was reading at the time. *Lorna Doone*, *East Lynne*, or a pathetic story about a Victorian child who was always ailing and who addressed her parent as 'Darling Papa'. I even made up Hiawatha-like poetry about nothing in particular which went rambling on without ever coming to a full-stop.

> See the shepherd, noble shepherd,
> With his dogs called Jed and Jess. . . .

My literary talents were sometimes put to the test when we played a communal game of Consequences round the dining-room table on a winter evening when company was present.

The others could always tell which were my contributions because of the bad spelling and the fact that I had not the gumption to disguise my handwriting.

Once, however, I was surprised to receive a word of commendation from the minister when we each tried to compose a verse in praise of the Borders. My father, I remember, wrote a funny one, but mine was dead serious.

> The Borders is a bonnie place,
> I wish that you could see it.
> England and Scotland look on its face,
> For ever blessèd be it.

'Not bad,' said the minister, patting me on the head, 'for a wee lassie.'

'She'll likely have copied it from somewhere,' said my mother, cutting me to the quick.

It was soon after this, I think, that I decided to run away from home. Nobody understood me – the age-old plaint – but I would make them sorry.

It was a pity it was not snowing at the time for my head was full of *Lucy Gray*, and I pictured my distraught parents following my footsteps through the snow and finding my frozen body. What remorse they would feel, and how I would gloat, gazing down on them from heaven!

But it was only raining. I set off in the direction of the Heathery Hill. I had never been beyond it. Indeed, there was nothing beyond except another hill and then another, all part of the Cheviot range. Not even a rainbow in the sky to follow.

It was a rough trudge and the backs of my legs soon began to ache. Before long I had an empty feeling in my stomach for I had not thought of bringing anything with me to eat. Gradually I began to long for the comforts of home and to forget why I was running away.

I sat down on the wet heather to consider my position. There were two alternatives. To run away, or to return home.

I looked back at the faraway farmhouse with the smoke curling up from the chimneys, and then at the bleak hills ahead. There was little doubt which was the more attractive.

It was the thought of a book that turned the tables. I was in the midst of reading *David Copperfield* at the time and could visualize it lying on the kitchen dresser where I had left it. It would be a pity not to finish the story, sitting comfortably on the rug before the fire.

No one had noticed I was missing. When I crept in, wet and weary, everyone was bustling about in the usual manner. *David Copperfield* was waiting for me on the dresser, and my mother was dishing up succulent kippers from the frying-pan.

'Take off your wet coat and sit in to your supper,' she said, giving me a passing smile.

How good and kind she was, I thought, changing my mind in midstream as I so often did. What on earth had made me want to run away? Never had a kipper tasted better nor my family seemed more lovable. How lucky I was to have such a good home and such an interesting book to read!

7. Suffer the Little Children

I used to stare at it every Sunday in the church. The stained-glass window opposite our pew. It was all dark reds and purples, making up a composite picture of the Good Shepherd in a long white robe, like granny's goonie, carrying a woolly lamb under his oxter. In his hand he held a long crook, like Jock-the-herd's, and at his feet sat some children looking up at him. They, too, were dressed in nightgowns.

The words underneath were difficult to read, but at last I deciphered them. *Suffer the little children.*

Who was doing the suffering, I wondered? The Shepherd or the children? Maybe the lamb? Sometimes the sun came shining through the window, brightening up the colours on the glass and transforming the Good Shepherd into a glorious angel all glowing with light. It was a great contrast to the stark kirk with its hard seats and its air of Sabbath gloom. I knew well enough who was suffering in our pew!

There was no hope of staying away unless one was seriously ill. From his vantage-point in the pulpit the minister noticed everything and counted all the heads, almost like marking the register. Even when he was praying he could look through his fingers and keep an eye on us.

Every Sunday rain or shine I had to walk the same two miles that I trudged to school during the week. But how different it was on Sundays. For one thing I was dressed in my best. I thought it strange that Jesus always wore plain garments, yet we had to tosh ourselves up when we went to worship him. In my case it was my good coat, buttoned boots, hat with elastic under the chin, muff hanging round my neck, hair tightly plaited, all adding to the general feeling of restraint. For another, the rest of the family was with me, the grown-ups keeping a stern eye in my direction and calling me to heel now and again, like a disobedient puppy.

No rushing from one side of the road to the other. No jumping in and out of the ditch. It had to be a straightforward walk with no deviations. Especially on the main road when we met in with other church-goers who engaged my parents in conversation, all matter-of-fact and dull.

Sometimes they looked at me and said, 'My! isn't she growing?' as if I was a plant in a pot.

I used to scowl back at them and think of all the things I would have liked to say. 'My! aren't you getting fat? That hat doesn't suit you.'

Even when I met in with other children we never dared kick stones or indulge in any of our everyday ploys. The boys looked uncomfortable in their tight breeks and the girls self-conscious in their Sunday hats with gloves on their hands. Suffer the little children.

The solemn sound of the kirk bell always made my heart sink to my buttoned boots. So did the sight of the churhyard with its moss-covered stones, some leaning sideways. There were always a few rooks cawing a dismal dirge from the nearby trees. (Where were the cheerful birds who chirped at me on week-days?) And at the door stood the elder in his decent black suit, guarding the plate and looking as solemn as if this was the Day of Judgement.

It might be the gamekeeper or a neighbouring farmer, but they could have been made of stone. No friendly chat, only a brief nod as I extracted my penny from my muff and placed it in the plate. Then in I went to the encircling gloom.

We all marched with measured tread to our pew, took our places and bowed our heads for a moment of silent prayer. I never knew what to pray for except that I wished it was all over. Usually I peered through my fingers to see who was already there. The Good Shepherd, of course, and Jessie, Joo-anne and Jock-the-herd who sat across from us, all three bolt upright with set expressions on their faces. The Sabbath look.

It was only when he was in church that I could see Jock was as bald as a billiard-ball. For the rest of the week his fore-and-aft bonnet was never off his head, but on Sundays he wore a bowler which he was forced to take off before entering the sacred portals. As he sat down in his pew after the exertion of walking, the steam rose up in a little wisp from the top of his bald pate, like a volcano about to erupt. I watched it, fascinated, till it died away.

There was plenty to watch as the congregation came trickling in, some with shoes that squeaked with every step they took. I knew everybody's Sunday hats and coats. Bella Confectionery had a velvet hat with artificial cherries that looked good enough to eat. Mrs Scott wore a fur tippet round her neck, like a little weasel with its tail clasped in its mouth. My mother wore a veil with little dots on it, and sometimes a feather boa: and the minister's wife always turned up her costume-jacket to keep it from creasing against the back of the pew.

Some of the men carried lum hats as a kind of status symbol, and walking-sticks or rolled umbrellas which they left in the stand at the end of their pews. They all wore tight collars and kept on their overcoats for the kirk was cold as well as gloomy. But we were not here for comfort, but to consider our sins.

There was an air of expectancy when we heard the side-door leading up to the laird's Gallery being opened. If the laird himself was in residence at the Big Hoose he sometimes brought his guests to worship in their special eyrie above our heads, even though they might be of different denominations.

I remember how surprised I was when I saw one of them going down on his knees to pray. But he was a Pisky.

> Pisky, Pisky, A-men!
> Doon on your knees an' up again.

We were Presbies and much more rigid.

> Presby, Presby, dinna bend!
> Always sit on your hinnerend.

The laird's party always entered last, like royalty; and when gentry was present the collection went up by leaps and bounds. Sometimes even a golden sovereign would be found in the plate. Piskies paid a lot for their religion.

It was not the done thing to look up at them but how could we help it? When we heard the rustling and the footsteps we tried not to turn our heads, but in the end everybody did. Often I saw Sir James Barrie perched up there like a little gnome, and Lady Somebody swathed in furs with a fascinating mauve-coloured toque on her head. They were all blue-blooded. Even some related to royalty. Breathing the same air as us!

After ringing the church bell, Wattie the beadle went round to the vestry and came marching in to the body of the kirk, bearing the big bible. He mounted the pulpit stairs, set the book in its place, then descended the steps and disappeared through the side-door leading to the vestry. After a decent interval he came back again with the minister behind him dressed in his long robes and with his hands clasped piously in front of him. Wattie waited till His Reverence was safely ensconced in the pulpit, then hurried up the little stairs and shut him in. It was a ritual that never varied Sunday after Sunday. I wished that either he or the minister would tumble down the stairs once in a while, just to create a diversion. Or that the minister would shut in Wattie by mistake.

The only variation was when the minister had to read out the announcement of a forthcoming wedding. Calling the banns. It was no surprise; everyone already knew about it, but it was exciting to hear it confirmed from the pulpit.

'There is a purpose of marriage between George Rutherford, bachelor, and Mary Briggs, spinster of this parish.'

The spinster sat in her pew with bowed head as if ashamed of herself, and the bachelor turned bright pink when his name was mentioned.

Miss Todd played the American organ with great gusto, pedalling away for dear life as if she was riding her bicycle. Some of the hymns were good-going shout-y ones like 'Onward Christian Soldiers' and 'Shall We Gather at the River?'; but the psalms and paraphrases were dreary and went on forever-and-ever. It was difficult enough looking them up with their confusing Roman numerals; and I could make little sense of the phrasing of some of the verses.

> That there is not a God the fool
> Doth in his heart conclude.

Even with all my lessons in parsing it was not easy to extract the meaning from such ramblings.

Iniquities I must confess
Prevail against me do;
But as for our trans-gress-ions
Them purge away shalt thou.

The psalmists seemed to take it for granted that we were all wicked and full of trans-gress-ions. Only God was good.

Goodness knows what Jock-the-herd made of the psalms, but he mouthed the words like everyone else. Except Joo-anne who, being hard of hearing, just stared into space and kept her lips resolutely closed. My father was the best singer in our pew, though sometimes he did not bother about the words and just sang 'la-la'.

Miss Todd set the pace, trying to keep the congregation from droning and dragging. Now and again she pulled out stops with strange words like *Vox Humana*, or pushed them in, and pedalled faster to get up more steam. But if we were walking through death's dark vale she would quieten us down to a sad whisper. The last verse was usually the loudest and most cheerful, promising us a place near the golden throne beside all the bright and glorious spirits clad in white array, and ending with a triumphant 'A-A-A-A-MEN!'

During the Long Prayer the minister gave God his orders, after first thanking him for our daily bread and other bounteous gifts.

'Help the sick, O Lord. Comfort the bereaved. Look after the poor. Bless our sovereign King and all the royal family. Give wisdom to those in authority over us. And finally, have mercy on us, thy humble servants.'

I wondered if God was sorting it all out and writing it down in a golden jotter, and if he would manage to get through it all. It would take him ages. And what about all the other prayers that were winging their way to heaven at the same time? How could he listen to the lot and do what every preacher told him? But, of course, God was omnipotent and it would be no bother to him to do a hundred things at once.

It was more difficult for me to turn up the right chapter in the Bible when the minister gave out the readings. Revelations was easy enough being right at the end, and Genesis being right at the beginning; but Ezra or Malachi were nuisances. Sometimes I was still wetting my finger and rustling through the pages when the minister said 'Amen' and shut the big bible. Often I just pretended I was at the right place and let the great mouthfuls of words wash over me.

It was a strange language but I liked listening to it. 'Verily, verily, saith the Lord'. The *Blesseds*, too, had a fascination for me, but I did not really listen intently enough to sort out the meaning, except when it was a parable which told a story. Though sometimes I tried to guess which sentence the minister would single out for his text. It would be somewhere in the two readings, from the old Testament or the New, and he would go over it again and again during the course of his long sermon.

It might be 'Blessed are the meek', or 'Six days shalt thou labour', or something about the Children of Israel. Never anything about the Children of Edgerston. It would have been nice, I thought, if he had spoken about something local for a change. But, of course, we were not in the bible.

The only time the minister mixed the secular with the sacred was when he stood up with a little bit of paper in his hand and said, 'I have the following Intimations;' but often they, too, were about church affairs.

'A retiring-collection will be taken for the Schemes of the Church' or 'Will the office-bearers stay behind after the service for a short meeting in the vestry?' But occasionally it was something special, like the announcement of a Sunday-School picnic or a Sale-of-Work. 'All contributions welcomed by the stall-holders.'

When he gave out the text there was a great rustling and coughing as everyone settled down, with looks of resignation on their faces, to thole the long discourse as best they could.

This was the moment when I longed to get up and bolt out of the door, but we were all prisoners, trapped in the House of God.

Some stared fixedly at the preacher and even cupped their ears not to miss a single word. Others slunk further back in their seats and unashamedly went to sleep. Jessie, upright as ever, never batted an eyelid, but sometimes she gave a jolt and I knew fine she was sleeping with her eyes wide open. But if Jock-the-herd slumped by her side she was always quick to rouse him with a sharp dig in the ribs.

At the start of the sermon there was much furtive passing of sweets along the pew. I was allowed one pandrop which I could either suck to make it last or scrunch and get rid of in one quick swallow. After that there was nothing left to hope for, unless the Maiden Ladies who sat behind me gave me a gentle tap and passed over an extra-strong in a gloved hand. This was a flat brown sweet so nippy that it brought tears to my eyes, but it kept me warm, if nothing else.

Jock once took out his pipe by mistake and was about to strike a match when he realized the error of his ways, but it was not often we had such a diversion.

Like everything else about the service, the sermon followed a rigid pattern so that there was never any surprise in it. The minister always divided it into heads: Firstly, Secondly, Thirdly, and Finally (Oh! how I longed for Finally)! He began quietly, then gradually worked himself up till he reached a crescendo, flailing his arms about and declaiming passionately about heaven and hell.

At times he seemed in a perfect fury of rage, very unlike the genial man who danced the polka in our kitchen when he visited us; and I was reminded of a story my father told me about the little boy's first visit to church. He watched in awe as the preacher thumped the bible, roaring like a bull at the congregation. Then he cooried closer to his father for protection and whispered: 'Faither! what'll we dae if he gets oot?'

It was strange to hear the minister addressing us all as 'My brethen'. Including Mary-Anne, and even me. Why not 'sistern'? I wondered. Usually I never listened at all except to keep a check on the heads, in the hope that he was nearing the end. I just stared at the Good Shepherd and thought my own thoughts, trying not to catch the eye of any of my schoolfriends who were inclinded, through sheer boredom, to make funny faces at me.

Bob (the braggart) had a habit of holding his breath for as long as he could and then expelling it in a great gusty sigh. I used to watch him getting redder and redder in the face and wondered if he would explode. It must have been a penance for such a stirring laddie to sit still for so long without even a catapult to play with.

Yet, though I never understood the sermon and considered it a wearisome endurance test, I felt there was something satisfying about the enduring words that went echoing round the church. Words I would never forget. Lo! I am with you always.

But the word I liked to hear best was Amen at the end of the sermon. There was a great rustle of relief when the minister finally uttered it and sat down with his face buried in his hands, before getting up to announce the last paraphrase. We sang it with great abandon, happy in the knowledge that release was at hand, and could hardly wait for the benediction before hurrying out into the open air. If God was watching he must have thought us very anxious to escape from his presence.

Never had fresh air seemed fresher than when we emerged from the kirk. I used to gulp it down in mouthfuls as if I was drinking wine.

We stood back respectfully at the door till the laird and his party took their departure. Sometimes he shook hands with my parents and introduced the Honourable Somebody to them before driving away in his large motor with the chauffeur at the wheel.

Even then the young folk could not run about or jump as we longed to do after sitting still for so long. We still had to hang about in a decorous manner in the background while the grown-ups indulged in their after-service talk.

This 'kirkyaird clash' was part of the Sabbath ritual. Now that God had been duly praised and the Children of Israel were safely across the Red Sea, biblical matters would never be mentioned again till next Sunday. The congregation came down to earth and discussed crops, the price of lambs, or any local gossip that was going. It was the one time in the week when they all got together and could exchange news and views.

Even Jock-the-herd, with his bowler shoved to the back of his head, leaned on his walking-stick and had a crack with some neighbouring shepherds. They all seemed different in their Sunday clothes and without their dogs at their heels. They never lingered long, not having much small-talk, besides being anxious to get back to their flock and into their old clothes.

Jessie never stopped behind but marched stiffly on ahead with Joo-anne at her side, her object being, as she once confessed to me, to get home as soon as possible so that she could take off her Sunday stays.

Though the women had more to say to each other than the men, they were the ones who broke up the kirkyaird clash and moved off first, thinking of the potatoes that were to boil for the dinner and the rice-puddings to heat in the oven. The men could follow at leisure, timing their arrival home when the meal was ready to be dished up.

The last to join us was the minister himself, transformed once more into an ordinary man. We walked as far as the manse gate with him, though I kept my distance just in case he banished me to hell. It was strange after all he had said in the pulpit to hear him talking about his cabbages and leeks with never a mention of 'Verily, verily.' Did he, too, lay aside religion with his dog-collar?

I tried to keep the text in my head till we reached Granny's half-way house, for she was sure to ask me if I had listened. I had to look it up for her in her own bible which was as fascinating as the one I found in the garret, with treasures hidden between the pages. Pressed flowers, scraps of baby-hair, faded photographs, and recipes for Christmas puddings. Granny would lay down her spectacles to mark the place and read the chapter to herself after we had gone. I was allowed a dip into the sweetie-tin and we would sit and chat with her for a while before walking the last lap home.

It was a relief to get rid of my Sunday clothes, but there were still some restraints. No rushing about or playing noisy games, no thumping on the piano, no quarrelling. 'Remember it's Sunday.' Everything was muted and low key. Even the cocks and hens seemed subdued and the bubblyjock went and brooded by himself in the cart-shed.

In the afternoon we went for a walk which I hated, for it was not a brisk walk but a quiet dawdle round the headrigs. This was a ritual on many farms, for Sunday was the only day when the farmer and his family could stroll together to take a look at the progress of the crops. Sometimes my father would stop to pick off an ear of corn and rub it between his fingers, or pull up a potato and examine the roots, while I kicked my heels in the background and longed to escape to my keep.

Sometimes I did escape. If I saw the herd making his way towards the lambing-shed, I fell behind and dodged over the dyke to join him. It was comforting to see Jock back in his everyday duds. But he still looked subdued, and in deference to the day never whistled through his fingers. The Lord, it seemed, did not like sudden noises on the Sabbath.

Last thing at night we sometimes had hymns round the

piano, with my mother playing 'Jesus Loves Me' and 'By Cool Siloam's Shady Rill', but they always made me feel faintly uneasy. I would sooner have had 'Stop Your Ticklin', Jock', and went yawning to bed looking forward to the normality of Monday.

All the same, looking back I can see the value of those long and seemingly dreary Sundays, not only because we had time to think of higher things in the kirk but also time to stand back and look at ourselves. Many a decision was made in the calm of Sundays. Small ones, maybe; even, in my mother's case, to put up fresh curtains next day, or, in my father's, to start cutting the hay in the morning. I made plenty myself, but seldom put them into practice. I would be good, like Queen Victoria; I would never lose another hair-ribbon; I would start writing a book about real people. My father and mother perhaps. But were they not too ordinary to write about?

It never occurred to me that grown-ups – parents especially – had private lives of their own. They were just there as focal-points for me. That was their function in life. To be parents.

My father, I knew, had to work on the farm in his guise as the boss and that he was out and about a great deal. I did not expect him to take much notice of me, but nevertheless I thought of him as 'Father' and nothing else.

I used to boast about him at school. The songs he could sing, the musical instruments he could play, the funny stories he told, the skill he had at games. Once, when he was passing that way, he appeared at the door to fetch me home in the gig. The master let me off without a murmur and came out to laugh and chat with my father, even helping me up into my seat. Never a word about: 'Hold out your hand!'

We said nothing on the way home. My father just whistled to himself and said, 'Get on, lass!' to Flora now and again. But I felt proud to be sitting there beside him and wished that I looked older and less tousled; then I might have called him

John, as my mother did, and discussed something sensible.

Normally, however, I saw less of him than of my mother. If she was missing when I came home from school I felt a sense of grievance. Where was she? Why had she not let me know that she would be away? When would she come back? Even though she never made much of me nor I of her, I liked to know she was there. She had no right to desert me without a word.

It had never seemed possible to me that my elders had once been young. So I was amazed beyond measure one day when my mother announced that she was having a school-friend to tea. I half-expected her to be wearing a gym-tunic and carrying a school-bag on her back. But she turned out to be as old and sedate as my mother herself. Except that when the two of them started talking they grew flushed in the face and giggled like young girls. 'Do you remember?' they kept saying to each other as if playing bat-and-ball, and went off into fits of laughter as they recalled some half-forgotten episode. What fun they seemed to have had away back in their young days!

Now and then they stifled their laughter, lowered their voices, and took a quick look at me. At last my mother said impatiently, 'Can you not go away and do something?' And though I felt aggrieved at first, I suddenly realized what a nuisance it must be to have inquisitive children straining their ears to overhear conversation not intended for them.

Then one day the pattern of life changed. I had assumed that it was set for ever, but now it would never be the same again.

Father drove away in the gig and came back with a stranger, a tight-lipped efficient woman who looked at me with cold eyes and said 'Shush!' every time I encountered her. She was a monthly nurse sent by the doctor. It had all to do with a baby which he was to bring in his black bag. For some reason my mother had to go to bed and stay there for a week or two while the nurse ruled the roost, demanding boiling kettles, hot milk, and little trays. She rubbed Jessie up the wrong way.

'Her! She's mair bother than a hunner bairns. Set her up!'

The doctor brought only one bairn. A wee boy as small as a doll, with a tuft of red hair, who squealed and squirmed as if he was unhappy with his new life and wanted back where he had come from. I thought he was not worth all the bother but my mother seemed pleased enough with him. Indeed, he took up all her attention and I was pushed further into the background while the nurse rustled up and down stairs, shushing me at every step.

At long last she departed. 'Guid riddance!' said Jessie when she drove away down the road in the gig, and I felt the same sense of relief that Jessie did when she took off her restricting Sunday stays.

Life more or less shook back into normal, except that I was no longer the youngest of the family and it was obviously the new baby who mattered most. Not that I could see anything special about him. He did nothing but sleep and cry.

Then one day 'the wee man' got all dressed up in his christening-robes – they had been mine, too – and the minister came and sprinkled water on his head from the silver rose-bowl. After that the excitement died down; but I felt myself more than ever an in-between.

I spent more and more time in solitary-confinement in the garret, or running about outside at the heels of the herd. Sometimes I 'helped' the hinds at haytime or harvest, riding home in the empty bogey at the darkening with my hair full of hay-seeds and my hands stinging with thistles. Jessie used to extract them with a large darning-needle. Thristles, she called them.

But it was at the sheep-shearing – the clipping – that I really came into my own. Even Jock thought so. 'Man-lassie, we'd never get on withoot ye,' he declared, and I believed him.

It was an understood thing that I could take French leave from school and next day just tell the teacher: 'Please sir, I was at the clipping.' It was a legitimate excuse for a farm-bairn, and better to tell the truth than conjure up 'a wee touch o' scarlet-fever' as one laddie did. And got skelped for his pains.

There was a great hustling and bustling in the kitchen beforehand as preparations were made to feed all the extra mouths. A number of neighbouring shepherds, some with Geordie accents from across the Border, always rallied round to help, and Jock would later repay them by going off with his shears to do a day's clipping in return.

Great roasts of mutton were sizzling in the oven. The biggest pots and pans were filled with potatoes, turnips, and cabbage; there were apple-pies for afters and scones and cheese to fill up the corners. Half-way through the morning my father brought out drinks for the thirsty clippers, and in the afternoon they gulped down cups of tea and ate soda-scones spread with rasp or blackcurrant jam.

It amazed me to see the amount of food the shepherds could consume at one sitting and to hear their unashamed belches as they patted their stomachs at the end of a meal. They sat in to the table in their shirt-sleeves while Jessie and my mother waited on them, and accepted everything that was set before them, never refusing second helpings.

At the end of the long hard day their backs must have been almost breaking after bending over the sheep for such a long time, and their wrists must have ached from wielding the shears. Yet they showed no signs of flagging, and set off cheerfully to trudge the long miles home. I never recollect hearing any of them grumbling about their lot. Only about the government when they discussed politics. 'A lot o' eediots.'

Our own herd was 'heid bummer.' For days he had been gathering his flock together, sorting them out, and shutting them into pens near the clipping-shed. The lambs, poor things, were bewildered and set up a dismal dirge when separated from their mothers. But: 'Hoots! ye'll a' get thegither later on,' Jock assured them as he cleeked a straggler round the neck with his crook.

A long trestle-table had been set up inside the shed at which Jessie, in yet another of her roles, presided. Her job was to roll up the newly-clipped fleeces into neat bundles, which she did with a few deft twists and turns. At the end of the day a big fleecy mountain had been built up in a corner of the shed to be sold later to the wool-merchant. But not before I had climbed it and tumbled about in its soft billowy depths.

Jessie's job was important but nothing compared with mine, for without my efforts I was convinced all the sheep would have been lost.

8. Tar-baby

The herd had lit an open-air gypsy fire outside the shed beside which I hovered expectantly. Over it he had hung a little tar-pot into which I dipped the branding-iron stamped with my father's initials. Any sheep that strayed from the farm could be recognized by the initials and sent safely home. All because of me!

I stood there waiting for the call of 'Buist!' which was the shepherds' way of letting me know that they had finished fleecing the sheep and that it was now ready for branding. The moment I heard it I dipped the branding-iron into the pot and carried it carefully to the caller, waiting till he twirled it round to get rid of the excess tar and imprinted the initials on the snow-white back of the shorn sheep.

All day long I trotted backwards and forwards answering the call till my bare legs were streaked with tar and 'Buist!' echoed in my dreams that night, mingled with the click-clack of the shears, the bleating of the frightened sheep, and the sudden bursts of talk and laughter from the men.

If only I had been a musician I could have composed a concerto out of the day's sounds, all mingled together into a continuous chorus. The Sheep-shearing Symphony. But at least I noted everything and tucked the information away at the back of my mind. Perhaps I could compose a word-picture of it some day if I ever learned how to become a writer.

It was fascinating to watch how the herds caught the sheep round the neck before turning them on to their hunkers and clipping the fleeces off in one complete whole, like peeling an apple without breaking the skin. Sometimes they stopped to sharpen their shears, to ease their backs or to light their pipes. There was a great deal of chaffing and now and then a loud burst of laughter or a snatch of song. Jessie was the target for their badinage but she gave back as good as she got while still continuing at her task. Nothing could put her 'aff the stot'.

Listening to the men's heavy-handed compliments ('Ay, Jessie, ye'd mak' a guid airmfu' ') I wondered if anyone had ever been sweet on her. She was handsome enough, a lot finer-looking than some of the herds' wives. So why had she never become a wife and had bairns of her own?

Suddenly I realized how little I knew of her inner life. Or anyone's for that matter. Borderers seldom bared their souls. Jessie's especially was as closely clamped as if she was always wearing her Sunday stays. But surely she had a secret Me, the same as I had. What did she think about when she was out in the fields doing her solitary tasks? I would have liked to listen in on her private wavelength. My own thoughts never stopped, but they were all a rag-bag of rubbish which needed sorting out. Though I had little time for private conversation with myself during the clipping with so many calls of 'Buist!' directed at me.

I was surprised to find that Jock-the-herd, usually so taciturn, had a hidden sense of humour which sometimes came to the fore when he and his cronies foregathered. Obviously he needed the right spark to set him off.

'Come on, Jock,'. they would urge him. 'Gie us a guid bar.' (A bar, I discovered, was a pawky joke.)

The herd would shake his head and protest, 'I dinna ken ony.' But presently his shoulders would begin to shake with silent laughter. 'Come on, man, get it oot,' the others would encourage him. And at length Jock would launch forth into one of his bars.

'A'weel, ye see, it was like this . . .'

It was difficult for me to pick up the thread of the story with so many distracting sounds all around. The dogs barked, the sheep kept up a ceaseless plaint, and the sharp shears made staccato snips as they steadily clipped away the wool. But it did not matter. What I was waiting for was the moment when the other herds would throw back their heads and explode into great roars of laughter. There was nothing half-hearted about them. If they were going to laugh they did it all-out.

'Man Jock, that was a grand bar,' they said approvingly, and thumped him on the back, after which he relapsed into his customary silence and it took a great deal of coaxing before he could be induced to say another word.

I could sense the feeling of cameraderie amongst the men, though now and again the old rivalry reared up, more in fun than in earnest. The Scots herds would have a sly dig at the Geordies, who were able enough to defend themselves in any verbal battle. It was comical to hear them trying to mimic each others' accents and attempting to sing each others' songs.

They showed due respect to my father, the Boss, when he came out to speak to them and bring them their drinks, but there was no touching of forelocks. We were 'a' Jock Tamson's bairns'.

Their attitude to me, as I see it now, was one of amused tolerance. I had not yet learned how to counter their bantering compliments. Indeed, I believed every single word they said, so that by the end of the day my head was in danger of being turned. Unaccustomed to flattery, it was a heady experience to be told I was a wee champion, the best 'Buister' in the Borders.

It took days for me to come back to earth and to erase the tar from my legs. And every time I saw one of the shorn sheep in the fields with the initials clearly stamped on its back I felt a stab of pride. *I* was responsible for that.

But I had to take a back seat at the lamb sales.

Again, it was Jock-the-herd who was in charge. For days beforehand he had been busy with the lambs, 'dickeying them up', even to the extent of powdering their noses as if they were Beauty Queens. It was important that they should look their best and fetch a good price, not only because it was vital for my father's pocket but also as a matter of pride to Jock himself.

In the early days Jock walked all the way to Hawick where the sales were held, driving the lambs in front of him and taking his time so that they would arrive looking fresh. It was a two-day journey. At night he put up at a half-way farm where the lambs were let loose in a field, and Jock kipped down in a bothy. These were the only nights, I imagine, that he had ever spent away from home.

There are still many side-roads in the Borders, drove-roads which the shepherds used when walking their flocks to market. Later, they were whisked to Hawick in great motor-trucks, arriving according to Jock, 'A' shoogled up'. He declared that the old way was better for the beasts who reached their destination looking 'mair like theirsel's'.

Jock preferred everything to be natural. Food, for instance. He would never eat a banana. 'If the Lord had intended me to eat bananas he wad hae grown them in the Borders.'

He used to tell me of the plain fare on which many hill shepherds existed, living alone in isolated cots and doing for themselves. They used to cook a great potful of porridge, enough to last a week. While it was still hot, they poured it into an empty drawer where it solidified. Every day they hacked off a lump and carried it with them to the hirsel.

I shuddered at the thought of it but Jock said, 'Hoots! it did them nae hairrm. I've kent drainers tak' a pickle oatmeal in their pooches an' when they were hungry they just cleaned their spades, sprinkled the meal on't, added a wee tait saut an' mixed it wi' waitter frae the burn.'

The habit of spreading both butter and jam on bread or scones had not yet reached our side if the Border, though I was introduced to it on my occasional visits over the Carter Bar.

'Nane o' your heathenish customs here,' Jessie reprimanded me when I tried to follow suit. 'It's ane or the t'ither. Ye'll ruin your stamoch.'

Jock's stomach survived his visits to the sales, though he came back both mentally and physically exhausted.

'Sic a dirdum!' he would say to me, leaning against a dyke. 'Folk! They mak' mair din than sheep. Ye can keep toons!' But if the price had been good he was justifiably proud. 'Ay! we bate Stotfield an' the Tofts. No' bad.' It was a feather in his cap as well as good money for my father.

On the few occasions when I was allowed to accompany my parents, driving all the way to Hawick in the gig, sometimes with Ginger between the shafts, sometimes with Flora, it was like going into another planet. No wonder Jock was bewildered with all that was going on. At the sale-ring, the noise was deafening. Sheep bleating, dogs barking, men shouting, the auctioneer keeping up a constant flow of talk, not one word of which I could understand. At the end of the transaction the farmers gave luck-pennies to the buyers and shook them warmly by the hand. It was sad to think of the sheep going off with strangers to be packed into railway-trucks and taken away to farms 'down England'.

The great moment came when Jock weired in our own sheep and kept them going round the ring to show off their paces. I felt the tension mounting in my father as he listened to the auctioneer and watched the bidders. If it had been shepherds who were being sold instead of sheep, I would have bid for Jock. He was the best-looking of the lot, in my opinion, with his bright red face and straggly whiskers. He must have been nearing sixty, but never mind! he was my ideal of man-hood.

When the last sheaves of corn were gathered in many farms in the neighbourhood held harvest-homes which they called kirns (not to be confused with the kirns in which they churned their butter). These jollifications were held in empty granaries, swept out and garnished with greenery for the occasion. A kirn was a free-for-all with everyone on the farm and their invited friends making merry. There was singing, dancing, plenty of food, drink, and 'guid bars'; and no one thought of going home till daylight.

I have a hazy recollection of attending my first kirn at a neighbouring farm, of the cocks and hens flying up into the rafters, of someone sprinkling soap-flakes on the floor to make it slippery enough for dancing, of Wat-the-Fiddler and a wee man with a melodion sitting up on a dais, of having to waltz with an enormous farmer unsteady on his pins, of falling asleep during a long Bothy Ballad and wakening next morning in my own bed, not sure if it had all been a dream.

Looking back, I often wonder if any of it was real. Not just the kirn. It is all so far away and long ago, how can the edges help being blurred like a faded photograph? And by now I have become so accustomed to conjuring up story-book characters out of my head that there are times when I doubt if Jock-the-herd ever existed outside my imagination. I have no photograph of him, but I can see him in my mind's eye as plain as porridge; and his drystane dykes are still standing on that windswept Border farm.

The creepie-stool on which I sat in the byre is tangible enough. I still have it in my possession, and the velvet pin-cushion with rusted needles sticking into it, which Jessie once gave me at Christmas. But the memories are less easy to grasp. Sometimes they fade away, overset by the more immediate happenings of here and now. Yet it only takes a small thing to bring them back. A whiff of tar and I can hear the clash of the clippers' shears and the call of 'Buist! Buist!'

If it was all a dream it was a very vivid one.

9. Jethart's Here!

The Golden Road to Samarkand could not have been more fascinating to me than the winding way that led to Jedburgh. The big town.

To me it was like getting a glimpse of the Promised Land; and the promise I made to myself was that as soon as I grew up and escaped from the mesh of childhood I would go and live there. Or, at least, to some big city where I could see something besides scenery. People in all their variety.

In those days I did not believe that there could be a town bigger than Jedburgh. I imagined it must be the capital of Scotland if not the world, with its High Street and Cannongate, its Abbey and Town Hall, its market-place and its shops. Not just one, like Bella Confectionery's, but dozens of different ones. Bakers, butchers, toyshops, newsagents, shoe-shops, sweet-shops, clothes-shops, even an Italian café which sold mouth-melting ice-cream.

It was the human beings, of course, who mattered most. I can just remember seeing Bobby the Bellman, the town-crier who lived in a mysterious place under the town-clock, emerging to cry the news, if there was anything urgent to announce.

He was a wizened little man, like a wrinkled apple, and the bell seemed too heavy for him to lug round the streets. He stopped at intervals to ring it before launching into his spiel.

'The water-rr will be turr-rrned off at four-rr o'clock for two hourrrrrrr-rrrs. You have been warr-rrr-rrned!'

His memory was not of the best. Sometimes he had his announcements written down on a piece of paper which he consulted every now and again while fending off a straggle of youngsters following at his heels. Their main objective was to snatch away the paper and put him off the stot. As Bobby grew more and more enraged and swiped out at his tormentors with his bell, his messages became more and more mixed up, till in the end he was almost crying with vexation.

When the pictures came to Jedburgh once a week it was Bobby the Bellman who went round the town calling out the title of the film to be shown. By the time he had traversed the length of the High Street 'the fill-um to be shown on Sat-urr-day' had changed its name several times, but at least Bobby always managed to convey the meaning, if not the correct title.

'It's something aboot an earrth-quake,' he would yell. 'Starr-ting at six o'clock sharr-rrp.'

The farmers had a special day when they gathered together in little groups in the market-place while their wives went round the shops. The shopkeepers welcomed the country folk, though money seldom changed hands. The grocer, the butcher and the shoemaker all knew that farmers had no regular income and were often short of ready money, so they allowed us to run up accounts and rendered their bills once a year, usually after the lamb-sales or the harvest. The bankers, too, were sympathetic to their country customers, knowing their fluctuating finances, and leniently lent them enough funds to pay their workers and tide them over the lean times.

My father, who was my banker, could always be coaxed to produce some coins from the depths of his pocket before going off to join his cronies at the market-place. With sometimes as much as threepence at my command the whole of Jedburgh was mine; but it was not the buying that mattered so much as the staring-in at all the treasures in the shop-windows.

The old name for the royal burgh and county town of Roxburghshire was Jeddart, or Jethart. 'Jethart's here!' had been the battle-cry of the men of Jedforest when they marched against their English foes. And in a history-lesson Auld Baldy-Heid had told us about Jeddart Justice. This, he explained, was the method used in Jedburgh in the old days, when a prisoner was hanged first and tried afterwards. Though this rough form of justice had happened so long ago, I was always a trifle apprehensive lest it might still apply, and took good care not to break the law, just in case.

I always spent some of my wealth on the local sweetmeats. Jethart Snails. All Border towns have their own specialities. Hawick Balls, Galashiels Soor-Plooms, Berwick Cockles. But Jethart Snails were the best!

I used to wonder why they were made in the form of snails. The reason, I was told, dated back to the time of the Napoleonic Wars, when a French prisoner was deported to Jedburgh and lodged with a family who sold toffee made in their back premises. It was the Frenchman who showed them how to twist the toffee into the shape of a delicacy from his native country; and so Jethart Snails were born, and are still being made today by the descendants of the same family. And I am still eating them!

Jedburgh, I also learned, had another link with France, this time through Mary, Queen of Scots. She had a fortress in Jedburgh – Queen Mary's House, now a museum – and it was here that she lay ill after visiting her lover Bothwell at the Hermitage, riding over moor and mire to visit him. In after years she said sadly, 'Would that I had died in fair Jedworth.'

But she did not die. It was her French chef who helped her back to health. In order to tempt her flagging appetite he concocted a dish made out of oranges or quinces, which the Queen found so palatable that it became a regular feature of her diet. It was given the name, so the story goes, of Marie-malade.

On my own more humble visits to Jedburgh my mother occasionally took me into a shop to buy a practical garment. A new coat perhaps. I was never given the chance to choose, otherwise it would have been a bright blue or a cheerful red, instead of a serviceable brown as it usually was. The main thing was that it should have a hem deep enough to let down, so there was little chance of getting rid of it for long enough.

Sometimes, too, I accompanied my mother when she went into the draper's to purchase curtain-material. She sat on a little chair by the counter while the draper, dressed in a black tail-coat and striped trousers as if he was going to a wedding, danced about from shelf to shelf, bringing bales of cloth to show her. She fingered the material, made her calculations, and he measured off the yards with his folding ruler before snipping away the stuff with a pair of sharp scissors.

After parcelling it up to be called for later, for my mother never carried any 'messages', he twirled the ends of his waxed moustaches and peered at me over the counter. I knew what was coming. Always some facetious remark, never anything sensible.

'So what mischief have you been up to lately? My! isn't she a swell in her Sunday hat! How would you like me to cut off your pigtails?' (Taking a lunge at me with his scissors.) 'Snip-snap!'

I was used to this kind of talk from my elders though I sometimes longed for them to take me seriously once in a while. Or that I could speak back and ask the draper the same kind of silly question. 'How would you like me to snip off your moustache? Snip-snap!'

I always tried to manoeuvre my mother into the newsagent's in the hope that she might buy me something to read, but usually there was nothing much on the counter except the *Jedburgh Gazette*, yesterday's *Scotsman*, or the *Christian Herald*; and if it was near Christmas I would get a preview of the new annual Santa would bring me. Little did I know there was a public library up the Castlegate or I would have made a bee-line for it, and never even bothered about the shops.

The baker's held a strange fascination for the farmers' wives, all such excellent cooks and bakers themselves. It was the difference, I suppose, that attracted them. They bought what they called fancy-bread (as opposed to plain bread), cookies, currant buns, parkins, iced cakes; and after a visit to town every frying-pan was sizzling with something tasty for supper which they had bought at the butcher's and fishmonger's. Sausages, kippers, or finnan-haddies.

The wives enjoyed encountering each other in the High Street, stopping to exchange news and swithering at the shop-windows before going in to try on a black straw or a brown velour hat. But buying a new costume was their biggest item. This was a ritual that required great thought and care, since such garments were made of everlasting material and could not be lightly discarded. Buttons were sewn on firmly, skirts were stoutly lined, hems could be turned up or let down, jackets had a timeless cut about them so that they could be worn for years no matter what the current fashion might be.

If it was to be a ready-made, it was easy enough to choose from the small selection available: the heather-mixture, the navy, the brown or the black. One farmer's wife who went all the way to Edinburgh to buy a costume was so perplexed when she saw the rows of garments on display that she returned empty-handed.

'I just could not make up my mind,' she declared. 'I was fair bamboozled. There were far too many to choose from.'

A tailor-made was a different matter, involving a long time spent in choosing the cloth, in getting measured and finally fitted. The result was a garment that was likely to last a lifetime, with each stitch firmly inserted and every pocket lined. I remember hearing someone bemoan to my mother, 'I wish to goodness my costume would wear out. I'm sick of the sight of it!'

Many things in the town surprised me; for example, that every door was shut and that each had a letter-box. Fancy! the people would never see their postie or invite him in for a cup of tea. The windows, too, were closed and curtained, with sometimes an aspidistra on display in a brass pot or a bunch of artificial flowers. They looked pretty enough but I would sooner had had some real bluebells.

Town-folk, I found, looked on us as a different breed, a little lower and less knowledgable than themselves. We were 'in from the country', not exactly savages, but people who lived strange lives at the back of beyond amongst the wild beasts.

'I couldn't stand it!' shuddered the woman in the baker's shop. 'All that dung!'

Yet they liked the pats of home-made butter and the fresh eggs brought in by the primitive country-dwellers, and were always remarking on our helathy looks.

The Jethart folk themselves seemed primitive enough when they indulged in a strange game on Handba' Day. This ritual was held every year to celebrate the coming of Candlemas. Any stranger passing through the town must have wondered if a battle had broken out, for all hell was let loose and it was a case of 'de'il tak' the hinmaist'.

What was it all about? The stories varied; but I was led to believe that the ball which was being kicked and flung around the streets represented an Englishman's head. Yet this was no longer a battle against the old enemy but between those born above the market-place and those born below. The Uppies versus the Doonies. The whole thing savoured of the Big Endians against the Little Endians. but the Jethart folk took it seriously enough and a blow-by-blow account was printed in the *Gazette* with as big headlines as if it had been the world war.

To my sorrow I was never allowed to join in, for the contestants were ruthless tacklers and a small child might get seriously hurt in the scrum. Nor were there any rules or referee. So I only saw it from a distance; and once I watched the combatants surge towards the river Jed and continue their struggle in the water, with the local swans joining in the fight, pecking out at Uppies and Doonies alike.

On normal days there was still plenty to see. Sometimes I went and gazed through the gates of the Grammar School. A forbidding building where in due course I would go to receive my Higher Education, if I managed to pass the Qualifying. It was an exciting as well as a frightening prospect. I tried to picture what it would be like to have so many classrooms and so many teachers. One for each subject, even French and Latin, instead of just Auld Baldy-Heid for everything.

Imagine coming to the big town every day! How would I get here? On horseback or on a bicycle? I had heard a rumour that they might run a school-bus if sufficient pupils from the country could be gathered together. But that was all away in the dim furture. Sufficient unto the day.

The Town Hall was the biggest building I had ever seen.

Something like Buckingham Palace, I imagined. I can remember the first time I was taken there as a special treat to see the moving pictures. This was magic indeed. It was enough to be in the Town Hall itself without the added delight of seeing a story unfolding on the flickering screen.

Sometimes there was a long hiatus when the picture broke down. The piano played louder and the children in the gallery stamped their feet and whistled through their fingers until Charlie Chaplin or Pola Negri reappeared to act out their dramas.

I hardly breathed or even sucked a snail, carried away by the entrancement of it all. The lovely ladies, the desperate men, the last-minute rescues, the loving embraces at the end. When it was over it took me a long time to come back to reality. All the way home in the gig I sat silent, thinking back over the story, wondering where the people on the screen were now and if they were living happily ever after. It was a great consolation to know that right triumphed in the end. I hoped it would be the same in real life.

If we stayed late enough in town I could watch the leerie going round the streets carrying his long pole. At his magic touch the lights sprang on one by one, transforming the grey Cannongate into a story-book street. The figures coming and going were not real people. They were characters like those in the film; and when they turned in through an open door they were not just going home to their suppers. They had gone in to rescue a lady in distress and to enact the next scene in some exciting drama.

People in towns must lead heightened lives, I thought, with such a variety of things happening all around them. How I envied them! It was not till we were bumping up the farmroad that the umbilical chord was broken and I began to look forward instead of back. Then the envy began to leave me.

Maybe it was the town-folk who were missing something in not having such cool clear air to breathe. They could not hear the hoolets hooting from the high tree or eat spare-rib for supper. Perhaps they were sitting hemmed in, in their tight little houses, longing for wider spaces and envying us who had come in from the country.

The far off hills are always greener.

10. A Day to Remember

I was not really aware of my surroundings until some far-away friends came to visit us and opened my eyes. They had come from the great city of London which seemed as remote as the moon to me and twice as romantic. So what could they find to interest them in a windswept farm with nothing to see but fields spread with dung?

Everything! Especially Auntie Gertie who went into ecstasies every time she saw a drystone dyke. It was the first time I had heard the word *picturesque* which she used to describe every single thing she saw. Even Jock-the-herd.

'Oh! look at the shepherd whistling to his dogs. Isn't he picturesque?'

Uncle Bob and Auntie Gertie were not real relations. Uncle Bob had been a childhood companion of my father's, and had taken the big step of going off to London to seek his fortune. He had found a job if not a fortune and made a 'mixed mar-

riage'. His wife was a neat little Englishwoman with a faintly
Cockney accent which I found fascinating though not always
understandable.

Auntie Gertie was a new species for me to study. Jessie
called her 'a dressy little body', for she was like a dainty wee
parcel all beribboned and tied up with bows. She wore little
boots with high heels, frilly blouses, and a belt that clasped
round her neat waist with a sliver buckle. Her hair was done
up in hundreds of curls, and she had more rings, brooches and
bracelets than I had ever seen before.

I just wanted to look at her and hear her speaking about
London. Did she know the Royal Family and what went on in
Piccadilly Circus? Were there really clowns there and performing elephants? Surely there were more picturesque things to see
in the big city than on our farm.

But Auntie Gertie did not think so. She went into raptures
over everything: the calves – 'such sweet little darlings' –
the clockers sitting on their eggs, and Jessie milking the cows.
Strangely enough, she and Jessie got on a treat though neither
understood a word the other said. Jessie even overlooked the
fact that Auntie Gertie was foreign. 'Puir wee body! she canna
help bein' English. But it's a peety she canna speak plain.'

It was funny to hear Jessie trying to teach the language to
Auntie Gertie. 'Bubblyjock!' she would say in a loud voice,
pointing out the turkey-cock. Then, even louder: '*Bubblyjock!*' She had no intention of learning anything from Auntie
Gertie. Let the English keep their own language to themselves.

Auntie Gertie enjoyed the wholesome farm fare and did such
justice to it that before she left the silver buckle would not
meet round her waist. 'Puir stervin' sowl!' said Jessie, as if
nobody ever ate any meals in London.

Uncle Bob was no stranger to the Borders. He had seen
everything before and was much more interested in recalling
bygone days when he and my father had been involved in
schoolboy escapades. They guffawed with laughter as they

relived the daft days of their childhood in Jedburgh. Sometimes I sat as still as a stone overhearing their tales of the time they stole the town-crier's bell, of how they painted a pig and sent it grumphing down the High Street, and of the day they climbed the clock-tower to try to alter the time. They were still boys at heart, I could see. What a pity they had had to grow up.

Sometimes I was squeezed into the gig beside them when they were taken for a drive around the countryside. The familiar places looked different seen through the visitors' eyes. What a lot I had missed before.

A kaleidoscope of pictures whirls through my mind of that illuminating visit. Because Auntie Gertie had an insatiable curiosity about everything I learnt more about Jedburgh than I had ever known before; that Bonnie Prince Charlie had once found refuge there; that Dorothy and William Wordsworth had lodged in Abbey Close; that Sir Walter Scott had visited them and read to them his new poem, *The Lay of the Last Minstrel*; that at Twonfoot Brig there was a pool in which the old women, suspected of witchcraft, were drowned.

One day we went to see the Eildon hills close at hand, passing by the village of Ancrum coyly hiding up a side-road, and came to Lilliard's Edge where, as Auld Baldy-Heid had taught me, the battle of Ancrum Moor was fought in 1545.

We stopped there to ponder over the sad fate of Fair Maid Lilliard who gave her name to the spot where she fell in battle attempting to revenge her lover's death. Auntie Gertie had tears in her eyes as she learnt off by heart the Fair Maid's touching epitaph engraved on the tombstone.

Fair Maid Lilliard lies under this stane,
Little was her stature but muckle was her fame;
Upon the English loons she laid mony thumps,
An' when her legs were cuttit aff, she fought upon her stumps.

On another day Flora trotted us all the way to Kirk Yetholm

where the gypsies lived. My father and mother often told the story of how, in their courting days, they had gone there together to attend the crowning of the last gypsy king, Charles Faa, whose name is said to have been handed down through a long line of kings from the Pharaohs of Egypt.

Crowds came from all parts of the Borders to see the spectacle. The royal procession arrived for the ceremony by means of a 'cuddies' quick-step' in a chariot drawn by six donkeys; and the king was solemnly crowned by the archbishop (in everyday life the local blacksmith) with a brass crown studded with imitation jewels. The band played 'Wha'll be King but Chairlie?' before the cuddies conveyed the monarch and his queen back to the tumbledown cottage which was their royal residence. It had been a great occasion, with bonfires and jollifications lasting far into the night.

On our visit we did not see His Majesty who was doubtless away round the countryside hawking pots and pans, but we did see his palace and some dark-skinned bairns who may, indeed, have been members of the Royal Family. Auntie Gertie was enthralled with it all, and squeezed so much pleasure out of everything that we all enjoyed it twice as much.

'Oh! look at that!' she was constantly exclaiming. Maybe it was just a fluffy chicken or a whin bush covered with bloom. Nothing special. But because of her enthusiasm I decided, even after she and Uncle Bob had gone, to keep my eyes open and look more closely at my surroundings. Not only places, but people.

The Mrs Things at the cottages, for example, the one perpetually shaking her rag rug and the other hanging out her washing. Maybe I could start a conversation with them instead of just saying 'Hullo' and passing by.

About what?

'It-it's a nice day,' I ventured, making a bold beginning.

Mrs Thing with the rug gave me a suspicious look through a cloud of dust, and the other took a clothes-peg out of her mouth to say, 'What's nice aboot it? Ye'd better hurry or ye'll be late for the schule.'

So I hurried by without continuing the conversation. But I had taken a good look at them for the first time; and what did I see? Faded blouses, long black skirts, stout brats tied firmly round their waists, red hands roughened and wrinkled through constant immersion in cold water, round fresh faces showing little expression except resignation. Or perhaps contentment?

Looking back, I wonder what the hinds' wives got out of their restricted lives, stuck in the wilds miles from anywhere. What if the women, living cheek by jowl with each other in adjoining cottages, hated the sight of each other? They had no one else to talk to while the men were working in the fields and never went anywhere except to church or maybe once in a long while to the local flower show.

True, it took them all day to get through their repetetive household tasks with no mod cons to lighten their loads. The women were forever carrying pails of water, feeding their hens and pig, black-leading the grate, rubbing and scrubbing, baking and cooking, mending and patching, pipe-claying their doorsteps or cleaning their windows. In their spare moments they knitted socks and jerseys for the men or long black stockings for themselves. Rarely did they take time to sit down and have a read at the paper or a look at the *People's Friend*.

Making meals, however simple, must have kept them occupied for hours. They baked floury scones, cooked rabbit-pie, and made great clooty-dumplings filled with currants. They got their milk and butter from the farmhouse, grew their own vegetables, and relied on the vanman or Wat-the-baker – when they could get up the road – for the rest. They saved up enough eggs to exchange for syrup and sugar in order to eke out the few pennies in their purses, and managed their frugal affairs without ever getting into debt.

On Saturday evenings the men sometimes dressed themselves

up and went cycling away to the town. Did the wives complain, I wondered, at being left behind? Or did they just cast on another sock? All of them must have had inner lives and secret longings. Surely it was not enough for them to be mere household drudges.

Certainly they could sparkle on occasions. One of my earliest recollections is of attending a wedding in one of the cottages. Whose wedding? All I can recall is a great feast set out on the table, of toasting the bride in ginger-wine, of the minister being solemn to begin with and them making comical remarks as everyone mellowed, of going to the door to watch the men taking part in the old custom of 'running the braes'. They set off at a brisk pace to race the measured distance and arrived back, breathless and panting, with the winner claiming a clumsy kiss from the bride who then presented him with his prize: a white silk handkerchief.

After that the jollification began in real earnest, though I saw little of it for my eyes would not remain open. But before I drifted off to sleep I heard the fiddle-music and saw Mrs Rag Rug kilting up her skirts to dance a schottische. She was wearing a lilac dress with sprigged flowers on it and a ribbon in her hair. Her cheeks were flushed and she was laughing like a girl. The other Mrs Thing was bouncing round the crowded room with the bridegroom, hooching in time to the music. She, too, had changed her personality with her clothes, and was all dimples and lace, with a gold pendant round her neck and shoes with pointed toes on her feet.

It was all so unlikely that maybe I dreamt it. Yet I am sure I heard the bridegroom stumbling his way through a speech, thanking my father who had doubtless supplied the wherewithal for the spree, and saying he was too full for words. My father sang 'The Lum Hat', and could it have been the minister who danced the sword dance with the poker and tongs laid out on the floor?

In my half-dreams I heard someone singing;

> Bessie Bell and Mary Gray
> They were twa bonnie lasses;
> They biggit a bower on yon burn-brae,
> And theekit it ower wi' rashes.

I wished the hinds' wives would wear their finery every day and dance instead of shaking their rugs. Why must there be such long gaps between high days and holidays?

But perhaps anticipation was best. It was nice to have something to look forward to. The flower show, for example. It happened only once a year, like Christmas, but we thought about it for weeks beforehand. It was so important that I could not understand why it was not on the calendar, like Ascension Day and all the rest.

'What aboot havin' a shot yoursel'?' Jessie urged me.

'Me? What could I enter for?'

There would be sports after the show and maybe I could enter for the sack race, but the show itself was for grown-ups who could grow the biggest cauliflower, make the clearest apple-jelly, or bake the best gingerbread.

We looked through the list of events, and true enough there were two things I could have a shot at. The best collection of wildflowers, and the best collection of wild fruits.

'An' what aboot this?' said Jessie, peering at the printed list. In the baking section there was an item which stated baldly: scones for spinsters.

'What's a spinster, Jessie?'

'Howts! you're ane! I'll pit on the girdle an' ye can hae a shot.'

My scones for spinsters ended in the pigs'-pail. Burnt on one side and doughy on the other, they were not fit for human consumption. So I turned my attention to the other items, and went racing all over the farm to collect as many varieties of wildflowers and fruit as I could find. I filled a jelly-jar with ragged robin, cats'-tails, silvery-shakers, star-of-bethlehem and all the rest, even ears of corn and barley-whiskers. I was not sure which were weeds and which flowers, but never mind, they made a brave show, though they began to wilt far too soon.

The thing to do with the wild fruit was to get an old tin tray, line the bottom with moss and make a pattern by embedding on it little heaps of hips, haws, rowans, barberries, brambles, acorns, scrogs and geans. It looked very colourful when it was finished. The trouble was, by the time it had been conveyed to the school (which, cleared of the desks, did double duty as the local hall) the contents were all shoogled out of place. No matter how carefully I tried to steady the tray as we rumbled down the bumpy farm-road in the gig, everything was a mixty-maxty mess in no time; and though I did a hasty tidying-up job I knew I would never win a coveted red ticket – and I was right.

It was surprising how eager the entrants were to win first prizes and how fierce the rivalry was between those showing their chrysanthemums, dropscones or hand-knitted socks. The prizes themselves were paltry enough. First prize 2s. 6d., it said in the catalogue. It was the red ticket that counted. Highly commended was no use. The judges who had been round the display earlier, tasting and examining, slunk away during the afternoon as if they feared being lynched. They could hear too many unflattering comments for their liking.

'Thon man's blind! Fancy pittin' a first on that cabbage. I wadna gie it to the coo.'

'Her! What does she ken aboot judgin' baking? Have ye ever tasted her ain sponges? Ye can hardly chowe them.'

'Three firsts for Mrs Scott! It's easy seen she's in wi' the judges.'

My father hated the occasions when he was called upon to be a Daniel and would have given everybody red tickets if

he could. But he, too, was as pleased as punch if his own
sweet-peas won first prize when someone else was judging
them.

It was suffocating inside the schoolroom, with the heat of
the people and the mingled scents of the goods on display,
the heady fragrance of the flowers, the sickly smell of the jams
and cakes. If the windows were opened bees came buzzing
in to sample the rasp jam and honey; and a felling of claustrophobia overcame me as I tried to push my way out against
the crowd.

The first time I saw anyone faint was at the flower show.
It was the minister's wife and I have reason to remember it
since she fell against me and knocked me to the ground; but
no one, of course, took any heed of me or my bruised leg.
They were too busy carrying her outside and propping her up
against the playground wall. It was the speak of the countryside for days, though she recovered quickly enough and even
took part in the three-legged race later on.

The sports were held in a field nearby on an uneven track
full of divots and thistles. There were other hazards, too,
between the starting and finishing-posts, for though the cows
and sheep had been ejected for the day they had left their
marks behind, and we had to be careful not to slither into a
cow-plat in the course of a race.

I liked the silly races best, the obstacle race, the egg-and-
spoon race, the sack-race, and best of all the thread-and-needle
race. It was fun to watch the men standing at one end of the
field holding needles at the ready while the women ran towards
them with long threads in their hands. The women pranced
about in a frenzy of impatience while the men tried to insert
the elusive threads through the eyes of the needles with their
clumsy fingers.

'Hurry up, Wull!' 'Get a move on, Tam!' urged the women,
helplessly watching their partners fumbling with the threads

and dropping the needles, while we all stood by kinking with laughter. A cheer rose up when some of them successfully completed the job, handed the threaded needles to the women who then raced helter-skelter towards the winning-post.

It was all very childish but: 'It fairly tak's ye oot yoursel',' said Auld Chuckie-Stanes, the roadman, when he came a cropper during the sack-race. That was the thing, to be taken out of oneself so that the humdrum pattern of everyday life was changed.

There were races for all ages and stages from small fry like myself to grown women. It was great to see Bella Confectionery running like a hen hotly pursued by Mary-Anne and Mrs Scott; but Jessie never took part in the races. 'Ye get mair oot o' watchin' ither folk makin' eediots o' themsel's,' she declared.

The men's handicap was the most hotly-contested, with everyone laying odds on the minister who was given a start half-way up the track, while the more able-bodied runners were left nearer the starting-post. Ready! Steady! Go! and they were off, with the onlookers yelling encouragement and the minister being overtaken when he stopped to retrieve his spectacles.

A great tea-urn was brought out to the field and refreshments were dispensed. There was fizzy lemonade for the young ones, and we ate all the gingerbreads and dropscones that had been on display at the show, whether they had won prizes or not. It was as good a way as any of getting rid of them.

The final event was the tug-of-war. The men took off their jackets, snapped their galluses and flexed their muscles before digging their heels into the ground to get a firm foothold. Then they spat on their hands and grasped the rope while the minister stood in the middle to start them off and see justice done. There were great groanings and gruntings as each side tried to stand its ground. In the end we all joined

in, tagging on at one end or the other and landing in a heap
on the ground when the rope gave way. It did not much matter
who had won as long as we had all enjoyed ourselves.

At the end there was a sweetie-scramble for the children,
with coloured jujubes and pandrops hailing down on our heads
like manna from heaven. We dived to the ground to retrieve
them, bumping our heads together and risking getting our
hands trodden on in our eagerness to collect as many as possible.
We stuffed them into our mouths, filled our pockets, and
clutched them in our grubby hands, searching amongst the
divots in case any had gone unnoticed.

It was a great day, one long to be remembered. But even
then the gaiety was not over. For the grown-ups, at least; for
now the schoolroom was cleared of its trestle-tables and wilting
flowers, the floor was swept and sprinkled over with soap-flakes
and a Grand Dance was held. Gents 1s. 6d.; Ladies 1s.

Being neither one nor the other but only a spinster of too
tender years for such orgies, I was whisked away home; but
in later years I made my debut at one of these country dances
and can still recall the thrill of anticipation I felt when I sat on a
long wooden bench beside the women, looking across at the
men and wondering if I would be 'lifted'. It never mattered to
me whether my partner was a ploughman with horny hands
or a young blood from over the Border. The main thing was
the joy of dancing, and not to be left sitting like a lone wall-
flower.

The music was provided by Wat-the-fiddler and a wee man
with a melodeon who played on till the sweat poured off their
brows. Every dance was so strenuous that before long the men
discarded their jackets and collars, and the dust rose up from
the floor and danced, too, in the air.

We always began with the Grand March, walking solemnly
round the room arm-in-arm with our partners. Then followed
the Circassian Circle, Petronella, Roxburgh Castle, Drops o'
Brandy, and all the rest, with an occasional schottische or

polka in between, or a round-about waltz to the tune of
'Come O'er the Stream, Charlie'.

There was never much conversation, for we had to reserve
our breath. Nor did the men bother to escort their partners
back to their places at the end of a dance but abandoned them
in the middle of the room the moment the music stopped,
before going back to sit on their own benches.

Half-way through, the great urn was brought into use once
more and cups of tea handed round to slake parched throats.
Sometimes a volunteer would do a turn or we would all join
in singing a bothy ballad. Then on with the dance till the
lamps flickered low, the fiddle-strings broke, and the dawn
chorus could be heard outside.

For weeks afterwards everybody spoke of the day of the
Show, savouring it in every detail. It was not just put
aside and forgotten, like the events in more crowded lives.
Looking back and recapping was often the richest part of
the fun.

Looking forward? There were long gaps between happenings. The only other social event I attended in the schoolroom was a whist drive where I won a string of onions as the
booby prize. I had only played snap before and was not too
sure which cards were clubs and which spades; but they were
short of someone to make up a table, and I was better than
nothing.

I was terrified most of the time, for there were some who
took it in deadly earnest as if they were playing for their lives.
Others chattered all the way through the game, not caring
whether they trumped their partner's aces. I felt proud if I
held some kings and queens in my hand especially if they were
'trumph'.

'What's trumphs?' the players wanted to know at the start
of a new game; and the master who was acting as M.C. called
out: 'Hearts!' or 'Diamonds!'. He rang a little bell when we
had to change places, but there were always some still swither-

ing over their cards before making the next move, as if they were poring over a draught-board.

Renaging – a strange word – was a deadly sin. I had to follow suit no matter how triumphantly I could have taken a trick by ignoring the rubbishy cards lurking in my hand. 'Can you not trumph it?' my partner would ask anxiously, and give a groan when I reluctantly produced my rubbish instead.

At some tables violent arguments broke out about who had played which cards, and sometimes the M.C. had to be called in as referee. His brow darkened, and I felt that at any moment he might bring out the tawse and wallop the lot of us.

The only time I had a good hand and took the most tricks was when he had called out: 'Misere!', but fortunately I was playing with Jock-the-herd at the time and all he said was, 'Man-lassie, ye couldna help it. Ye had the hale Royal Faimly in your fist.'

Next day the schoolroom was back to normal, with the blackboard filled with vulgar fractions and Auld Baldy-Heid shouting: 'Sit up and look lively or you'll get what-for.'

Once in a while the minister organized a social evening. A kirk soiree. This was a kind of congregational-meeting with some entertainment thrown in as light relief. It was strange to hear laughter, chatter, and hand-clapping in such solemn surroundings, with the Reverend in a jovial mood, telling funny stories instead of reading from Deuteronomy.

We had heard all his jokes before but they were none the worse for being repeated, and we dutifully went into fits of laughter as if they were all new to us. One I can remember still, for he retold it so often and with such gusto that I could have prompted him if he stuck, but he never did.

It was the story of a preacher who found himself face-to-face with a raging lion in the jungle. I could picture the raging lion all right, but I used to wonder what on earth the preacher was doing in the jungle.

'I'm going to eat you,' said the lion. 'Prepare yourself for death.'

What was the preacher to do? There was no hope for him. Except prayer. So he knelt down, put his hands piously before his eyes and prayed more earnestly than he had ever done before. Suddenly he keeked through his fingers and to his surprise and delight saw that the lion was kneeling, too, with his paws in front of his eyes.

The preacher looked up to heaven and said, 'Isn't it wonderful to think that my words can soften a wild beast's heart?' Whereupon the lion dropped his paws and roared: 'Haud your wheesht! I'm saying grace before meat.'

The highlight of the evening was bursting the pokes. We were all presented with paper-bags containing our feed, and a great feed it was, too; solid-looking meat-pies or bridies, hunks of cake or substantial buns with coconut-icing on top. Sometimes the contents of the pokes varied, and we compared them with those of our neighbours, occasionally swapping a cream cookie for a doughnut. But the great thing was to empty the bag as quickly as we could, blow it up and then burst it with the biggest bang possible.

We were also given handfuls of conversation-lozenges. In the dim light we peered at the heart-shaped sweetmeats to see what messages were written on them before passing them to someone of our choice. I remember handing: 'Will you be mine?' to the herd, and was a trifle dampened when he passed back: 'Not tonight', but I sucked it just the same. After that we settled down amongst the debris of crumpled paper-bags to enjoy the rest of the evening's entertainment.

The minister had imported some of his friends from neighbouring parishes who fancied themselves as singers or raconteurs. I remember a large lady and a small man standing up side-by-side to sing a duet, self-consciously avoiding each other's gaze as they launched into the song. It was a tear-jerker called *The Crookit Bawbee*, a touching tale of a love-token, a long separation and a reunion. Even though I knew the wee man would end up hand-in-hand with the big lady, they sang with such pathos and stirred my emotions to such an extent that I could scarcely swallow my lozenge.

I remember, too, the wife of one of the visiting ministers standing up to sing 'Won't You Buy My Pretty Flowers? with a bunch of artificial anemones clutched in her hand; after which her husband told a funny story – which he assured us was true, but I had my doubts – about one of his elders, a very shy man, who tried to avoid sick-visiting in case he was forced to 'put up a prayer'. The day came, however, when Mrs Brown, in his district, fell ill and he was sent off to do his duty, with instructions that he must pray at her bedside if she asked him to. He went off looking very down-in-the-mouth, but when he returned he was all smiles.

'How did you get on?' the minister asked him.

'Fine, meenister, fine! She was deid afore I got there.'

At the end of the proceedings we had to subdue our mirth and stand up to sing the Doxology. After which the minister blessed us, and we went home in the moonlight sucking the last of our lozenges.

11. Grasping the Nettle Firmly

Time did not seem to matter when I was a bairn. A day stretched into infinity and I never bothered about dividing it up into hours and minutes. The only watch I possessed was a toy one which came out of a Christmas cracker, but it did not go. So I just used to blow on a feathery clock and pretend I could tell the time that way.

There was a sundial in the garden but it was all covered over with moss, and we had a temperamental old grandfather clock in the hall which used to chime thirteen to the dozen, though never at the right hour. But if we were really stuck we could always ring up Bella at the post office. Not that she always knew.

'What are ye wantin' the time for?' she would shout down the receiver. 'I dinna even ken what day it is. But if ye haud on a meenit I'll gang ben the hoose an' tak' a keek at the wag-at-the-wa'.'

The trouble with Bella was she could never remember whether her wag-at-the-wa' was ten minutes slow or twenty minutes fast. 'It's roondaboot half past ten,' she would announce, 'but it micht be nearer eleeven o'clock, though I couldna sweir on't.'

Jock-the-herd had an enormous fob-watch which he kept shut up like a prisoner in his pooch, but it was a day's work to get it out, open it up, shake it to see if it was still ticking, and then peer at it closely enough to look at the time. Even then he had to do his calculations, for Jock, too, kept his watch fast. Or was it slow? In the end it was easier looking up into the sky and just guessing.

Jessie was the best at telling the time. She could feel it in her bones, she said. 'It's toonty past,' she would tell me; but toonty past what? 'Time ye were awa' to the schule.'

Sometimes we listened in to Big Ben all the way from London. He never made a mistake and chimed the wrong number. I used to picture him, a great fat man, sitting on top of the Houses of Parliament, hammering out the hours while I counted them off on my fingers.

The frightening thing was to wake in the middle of the night not knowing what time it was, alone in the world with not even a mouse stirring. The old hoolet outside sometimes broke the stillness with an ominous hoot, as if warning me that the Day of Judgement was at hand.

'Hoot-hoot! They're coming to get you. Hoot-hoot!'

Strange thoughts went whirling through my head about fundamental things which did not seem to matter in the bright daylight. Was God really up there watching over me? What if I died suddenly? Would Gwen, my friend, be there to welcome me or would she have forgotten all about me?

It would be terrible if I went to hell instead, into the burning fire. I thought over my sins, which were many, and determined to lead a purer life if I survived till the morning. My heart thudded when the wardrobe creaked as if it was alive and stretching its muscles. Something jumped on to my bed. It was only the white kitten. She lay on top of me purring as if she had an engine running inside her. Her presence was comforting, but the black thoughts still remained. There were a hundred questions I had never been able to ask anyone, but I would try in the morning. Maybe Jessie would tell me.

But, of course, it was all different in the daylight; and I was reminded of one of my father's stories about the minister who asked a small boy if he prayed night and morning.

'A'weel, I whiles pit up a prayer at nicht,' was the reply, 'but ony smert callant can tak' care o' himsel' through the day.'

All the same, I stuck to my purpose and tried to get Jessie to answer one of my questions.

'Jessie, where are we going to when we die?'

She did not hear me at first for she was stripping off the brown cow and the milk was rattling against the sides of the pail. But I persisted and repeated the question in an urgent voice.

Jessie gave me a hard look as if she was about to tell me to hold my tongue, but she must have realized from my expression that I was in deadly earnest for she gave me a serious answer.

'Naebody kens, lassie. We've just got to hope.'

It was a great thing, hope. My hope was that I might grow up to be good, not exactly a saint good enough to end up on a stained-glass window, but someone who might be a shining example to others. It was hardly likely at the rate I was going and with my lack of rummlegumption. But at least there was one person who thought I was perfect and in whose eyes I could do no wrong. Wee Maggie.

She was one of the hind's bairns, a toddler who used to haunt me like a shadow, hovering at the door, waiting to see if I would come out and play with her. She spoke with a lisp and trotted after me like a pet lamb, content if I threw her the odd word. She was a nuisance at times, but it was a heady feeling for me to have such a devoted slave, agreeing with everything I suggested, from turning somersaults to jumping across the burn.

'Oh yeth! Anything you thay!'

Wee Maggie was too young to go to school, so I sometimes showed off my superior knowledge to impress her, and tried to teach her to read or told her stories. She liked the stories all right but she was not so keen on the lessons. Sitting on a hay-rick I would go over the alphabet with her.

'Are you listening, Maggie?'

'Yeth!'

'Well, what comes after D?'

'I couldn't thay. Tell me a thtory.'

I found myself behaving like Auld Baldy-Heid and scolding her till her lip began to quiver. Great tears would well up in her eyes and drip down her cheeks like raindrops. Then I would feel ashamed of myself and hunt in my pockets for a consolation.

'Would you like a caramel, Maggie?'

'Oh yeth, pleathe!'

The tears dried like magic to be replaced by beaming smiles. It took very little to make Maggie happy, but I could never leave well alone. I was always trying to improve her.

'Would you not like to learn to count?'.

'Y-yeth!'

'Well, come on then. I'll teach you.' Clever me!

Poor Wee Maggie had to puzzle her brains over the two-times table, getting as far as: 'Ten two'th are twenty' before I gave her any peace. She only did it to please me and had forfotten it the next day, but it gave me a great sense of power.

Then suddenly I realized I was as bad as the grown-ups, demanding instant obedience. 'Go and fetch that ball!' 'Don't fidgit!' 'Stop biting your nails!' In fact, I was becoming a bully.

In a fit of remorse I went to the other extreme and grovelled before Wee Maggie, running and fetching things for her, giving her my hair-robbons, asking her advice.

'You choose, Maggie. What would you like to play at? Hide-and-seek?'

'Yeth!'

'Or would you rather play with the ball?'

'Yeth!'

She was eating a jammy-piece at the time and her cheeks were splattered with red-currant jelly. I had to stop myself from saying sharply, 'Wipe your face!'. Instead, I asked her, 'Which would you like best?'

'Anything you thay!'

It was obvious Wee Maggie was made to be a doormat and enjoyed being bossed. But I had to keep a strict rein on myself. What if I turned out to be a monster, like the Drilly, drunk with power?

'Watch it, you!' I kept warning myself.

I watched the animals, too, to see how they behaved and if they bossed each other; but with them it seemed to be a case of live and let live. Except, of course, for the bubblyjock who had all the worst characteristics of the Drilly, and more.

It was Jessie who suggested the right way of dealing with the bully one day when he came charging after me, trying as usual to peck at my bare legs.

'Stand up to him, wumman.'

'Oh, I couldn't, Jessie. I'm feart!'

'Awa'! He's feart for you.'

Jessie was always right but I found this too difficult to believe. The bubblyjock feart!

'He's just a beast,' scoffed Jessie. 'Turn roond an' gie him a gliff.'

The very idea! It was like facing up to the Charge of the Light Brigade. But if I was feart Jessie wasn't.

'Haud on an' I'll show ye.'

When the bubblyjock came running at us on his muckle splay feet she whipped off her apron and waved it in front of his face, shouting, 'Boo! Get awa', ye ugly brute!'

The bubblyjock stopped in his tracks and gave Jessie an astonished look. Then all the fluff seemed to go out of his feathers. The next moment he turned tail like a coward and ran away to hide under the reaper in the cartshed.

'See, lassie! Ye should aye gie a firm grip to a nettle.'

But it was a different matter trying it myself. I did not mind nettles, but the bubblyjock still terrified me even though I had witnessed his downfall. He soon recovered his equilibrium, waited till Jessie was out of sight, and renewed his attacks on me, while I tried to raise enough courage to fight back.

At last I did it. Trembling with terror, I braced myself and turned on him. I had no apron to wave but I shouted 'Boo!' in as brave a voice as I could muster.

Once more it worked like magic. The bubblyjock looked even more frightened than I was, and went scuttling away backwards gobbling his head off as if I was about to murder him.

After that I had the upper hand. Though he still tried to chase me, I always turned and chased him instead. It was a great step forward in my life. I felt I could face up to anything, though I still had not the courage to say 'Boo!' to the Drilly.

I wanted big things to happen so that I could try out my new-found bravery. If I had been living in the old days I could have brandished my battle-axe in the face of the enemy and fought, like Fair Maid Lilliard, on my stumps. It was a pity I was never tested or they might have put up a monument to me. I even made up my own epitaph.

> The one who lies inside this grave
> Was very small but very brave;
> She saved her country from the foe
> But what she did I do not know.

The last line was a bit feeble, I felt, but at least it rhymed.
The trouble was there was no foe to fight. One could not live on the heights all the time, and maybe it was not the big things that demanded the most courage, but doing the every-day dull things. Just keeping going; my trudging to school every day, the herd battling against the elements without a grumble, Jessie up to her elbows in soapsuds doing the weekly washing.

Sometimes I helped her, though in the end she declared I was more of a hindrance, getting so wet in the process that she often said, 'Ye're mair drookit than the claes. I'll need to wring ye oot when I'm feenished.'

But at least she admitted I was a help in keeping the boiler going. The washhouse was a draughty old building situated in the steading, open to the world so that ducks, dogs, cats, calves and other beasts came wandering in. The boiler was heated with firewood and was, according to Jessie, 'As fashious as a twa-leggit cuddy'. Either it would roar away like an inferno, if the wind was in the right direction, blowing great gusts of smoke into our faces and making our eyes smart, or it would take the sulks and have to be relit over and over again.

It ate up sticks so that I was kept on the trot fetching and carrying, while Jessie got busy with the scrubbing-board. Sometimes she used a long wooden poss to pound out the dirt; and once to my joy when she was doing the blankets she took off her clogs and stockings and got into the tub herself. I jumped in beside her, clutched her round the waist, and we pranced about on our bare feet as if doing the Highland Fling. It was a great feeling, the hot soapy water on my legs and the squelchy blankets beneath my toes.

Not such fun when it came to rinsing them and wringing them out. They were too thick for the wringer, so Jessie commandeered the current servant-lassie or the herd if he happened to be passing.

'Here! haud on to that end an' gie a twist.'

When the great wash-basket was full of clean clothes, I helped Jessie to carry it round to the back-garden where she hung the washing-line between two apple-trees. After pegging the clothes on the line she propped it up with long forked sticks and stood back to contemplate the sheets and pillow-cases blowing in the breeze.

'No' bad,' she would say with a certain amount of satisfaction; 'but ye'll need to keep an eye on the rain.'

That was my job, to keep an eye on the rain. At the first drop I raced round to the washhouse where Jessie was cleaning out the boiler and announced, 'It's spitting!'

Jessie never said bad words. She just tightened her lips and braced herself for the worst, which meant going through the tedious process of taking all the clothes down again, and later on, if the sun shone, pegging them back on the line.

When they were dry enough she spent hours ironing, pressing, and goffering them with the old box-iron before hanging the clean clothes on the winter-dyke to air. Sometimes she put her hand to her back and said, 'Eh whowh!', but she never said, 'I'm fed up!' as I did when I got tired of a job.

She would never be a heroine in the history-books, famed for her courage, but I felt that if anybody deserved an epitaph it was Jessie.

12. Growing Pains

My mother was a witch.

She often said so herself, in so many words.

'I am a witch.'

Not the kind who flew through the air on a broomstick or cavorted around with her coven. But she had flashes.

'I'd better do a baking,' she would say suddenly. 'I have a feeling the minister's coming to tea.'

And he came.

'See,' she would say, when he opened the garden gate. 'I am a witch.'

I often wished she would look into the future and tell me, in moments of indecision, what was the right road to take. But in did not work that way. I soon discovered that the most difficult thing in life was making up one's own mind. Even choosing between an apple or an orange could be a great problem, or having a whole penny to spend on sweets at Bella's shop. Having made the vital decision, it was always the other thing I wanted most. If only an inner voice could have advised me!

One year my mother had a flash just before Christmas.

'We're in for a snowstorm,' she announced in her guise as a witch.

No one believed her, since the big snows seldom came till after the turn of the year. But she was right. The storm came on suddenly and unexpectedly with none of the usual preliminary warnings. It started with a sinister silence followed by a flutter of snowflakes and an icy wind which later blew the snow into wreaths as high as mountains. We knew the pattern. Soon we would be enclosed in a white cocoon with no hope of anyone getting near us. So what about Santa Claus, in whom I still firmly believed? If the postie and the vanman could not reach our door, how would Santa find his way through such a storm?

I asked Jock-the-herd when he came stamping into the kitchen with his boots caked with snow.

'Och! he'll come,' Jock assured me, 'if ye shout up the lum. Santy'll no' let ye doon.'

So I shouted up the chimney. 'Santa! would you please bring me a book, and a dolly, and some sweeties.?'

I heard a noise at the chimney-top as if Santa was saying, 'Ay! I'm listening,' but maybe it was just the wind.

On Christmas Eve, before going to bed with my stone hot-water-bottle, I hung up my stocking and left some sustenance for Santa to revive him after his long journey. A glass of milk and a slice of gingerbread. I had meant to stay awake to greet him, but my eyes closed and I knew no more till morning when – oh joy! – I discovered that he had come. Not a drop of milk left in the glass, not a crumb of gingerbread. And he had answered all my requests.

He had brought me a book. Not the usual *Chatterbox* but an old volume of *Lamb's Tales* with a new cover on it. There was a dolly, too, made of rags and wearing a Red Riding Hood cloak over a dress of the same pattern as my old summer frock. He had not forgotten the sweets, though strangely enough they tasted just like Jessie's treacle-toffee. As an extra he had filled my stocking with crab-apples, a few nuts, and a stick of sugarally.

I could hardly wait to tell Jock-the-herd.

'Santa's been!' I shouted when he came in with an armful of sticks to keep the kitchen fire going, and proudly showed him my treasures.

'Man-lassie, I tell't ye', said he, looking pleased for my sake.

Then I asked him, 'Did he come to you, too, Jock?'

The herd looked a trifle uneasy. 'Santy? Och ay! I daursay he did.'

'What did he bring you?'

Jock waited till he was almost out of the kitchen door before telling me. 'A pair o' lang drawers.'

I thought it a strange present for Santa to bring and wondered if Jock had shouted up the lum for that. Later, I gave him some of my toffee as a consolation. As for Red Riding Hood she was my constant companion for many a long day. Though she was only made of rags I liked her better than any fancy doll who could walk, talk, and close her eyes. Indeed, Red Riding Hood's eyes were only buttons which fell out every now and again. Her arms, too, had to be sewn back on at intervals; but what I liked best about her was that she understood me and approved of everything I did. She shared all my thoughts and many of my gaol-sentences. With the older ones back home for the Christmas holidays and the new baby ruling the roost, I was thankful to have somebody of my own, even if it was only a rag doll.

I cannot remember that we celebrated Christmas in any special way with a party, except that we had a plum-pudding and ate the bubblyjock. The trouble about decorating the house was finding the holly. There was plenty of it around, great prickly trees grew in the wood nearby, but the scarlet berries ripened too soon, and those not pecked by the birds had withered long before Christmas. It was Jessie who had the bright idea about how to preserve it.

'Bury it ablow the grund,' she suggested, 'in an auld biscuit-tin.'

We bought our biscuits, like everything else, in bulk; and always had plenty of big tins at our disposal. So every year we gathered sprigs of holly laden with red berries, put them into the biscuit-tins and gave them a decent burial.

The problem was finding them again. We even set up little wooden crosses to mark the spots, but routing pigs soon knocked them down, and, of course, in a snowstorm there was no hope of retrieving the buried treasure. So, as often as not, we had no holly.

Hogmanay was a more special occasion, though we had no one to first-foot except the cottagers. Every year my father gave them the same presents: boxes of shortbread, a black bun, and a side of mutton. Sometimes they came and sang bothy-ballads to us in the parlour, or joined in a kitchen dance, ending with linked arms and everyone singing 'A Guid New Year To Ane An' A'.

Then suddenly the date changed. There were brand-new calendars to hang up. I had a feeling that I was beginning a fresh life and all my old sins would be forgiven.

One day my mother, gazing into her cup, said, 'There's a stranger floating in my tea. I wonder who it can be?'

All day long I watched and waited for the stranger. Could it be an Ingan Johnny or a French polisher or a wandering packman? It would not be the minister, for he was no stranger. I hoped it was not to be the Man from the Reformatory. For long enough he was my childhood bogey. I had no idea who he was except that my elder brother and sister were constantly threatening me with him. 'If you don't behave yourself the Man from the Reformatory will come and take you away.' I used to run and hide up a tree or in the stair-cupboard amongst the brooms any time an unknown man came near the house.

Nothing happened. For once the family witch had failed. I had almost forgotten about the stranger and was out in the stackyard skipping with an old length or rope when I saw him coming limping up the field. He was wearing a pink coat which grew pinker every moment from the drops of blood that were dripping on to it from a gash in his forehead. At his heels trotted a shamefaced horse.

I stared at him in horror, not knowing what to do or say. But he did. Indeed he seemed quite cheerful in spite of the blood on his brow and the bruises on his leg.

'Took a tumble at the hunt,' he told me. 'Do you think I could go somewhere, little girl, and get patched up?'

No one had called me little girl before or appealed for my help in such an emergency. I forgot my shyness. 'Come on,' I said and held out my hand.

Jessie was horrified when I led him straight into the kitchen instead of going round to the front door, and gave me a second scolding later on.

'Have ye nae rummlegumption? Fancy bringing the likes o' him into the kitchen!'

'It was nearer,' I protested; but evidently etiquette mattered more.

'Ye're a glaiket gowk!' Jessie told me. 'He micht be a lord.'

Whoever he was, my parents took charge of him, and after he had rested and been refreshed 'ben the hoose', he took his leave with a bandage on his forehead. But he insisted on saying goodbye to the little girl and thrust a silver coin into my hand. After that I kept looking in my own tea-cup for strangers, but I never saw any.

One day, however, I did have a flash myself. It was the day we broke up for the school-holidays. There was a relaxed atmosphere in the classroom. Auld Baldy-Heid had become quite human and was asking us all where we were going for our holidays. There were not many answers, for few of the country bairns went on holiday. They just ran wild, as I did, until it was time to go back to school again.

Only one or two put up their hands.

'Please sir, I'm going to stay with M'Auntie in Hawick.'

'I'm away to Kelso, sir.'

Kate, my friend from over the Border, said smugly, 'Please sir, I'm going to Newcastle.' Lucky thing!

Suddenly, without thinking, I shot up my own hand.

'I'm going to the seaside,' I heard myself announce.

'The seaside!' said the master in an interested voice. 'Where?'

'Please sir, I don't know, sir,' I said and subsided in my seat. Fancy telling a black lie like that!

The enormity of my sin weighed heavily on my shoulders all the way home. I had scarcely got into the kitchen before Jessie said, 'Ye'd better try on your new plimsols.'

'Plimsols?' I said in surprise. 'What for?'

'Ye're gaun your holidays to the seaside.'

It was a miracle, of course, like the ones in the Bible. If I had turned water into wine I could not have been more astonished. It was the opposite of be sure your sins will find you out.

The seaside to which we were going had the unpromising name of Spittal. It was near Berwick-on-Tweed and I was not sure whether it was in England or Scotland; but it did not matter as long as the sea was there.

We went in a train, a great snorting monster that belched out mouthfuls of smoke and sparks like a dragon, and rushed through dark tunnels with terrifying shrieks. The unfamiliar landscape kept running away backwards before I had time to examine it properly. I wanted to see everything more closely, even the tattie-bogles in the fields.

Then suddenly we were there. Spittal! I could see a cluster of red-roofed houses, a church spire, some coal-pits, but no sea. Our lodgings were too far away from the front, but it was there all right, and at last, in my new plimsols, I was taken down to the shore to see it.

I could not believe my eyes; there was too much of it. I had pictured the sea as a biggish pond which one could walk round or sail on in little boats. But this was beyond my imagination. The endlessness of it, stretching away beyond the horizon, confounded me. It was like eternity, which the minister talked about on Sundays. I wondered if it would spill over and drown the whole world.

It took a long time to get over my first fright or to venture as far as the water's edge. When I took off my plimsols and felt the sand falling away under my bare feet I felt sure it was going to suck me in. The waves folding and unfolding mesmerized me, and for long enough I resisted letting the salt water swirl over my toes.

But in time familiarity bred contempt. Soon I was wading up to the knees, and then, in breeks and vest – for I had no bathing-suit – I began bobbing up and down in the water and even let the waves splash over my head. It was a wonderful sensation; and I felt I could write a better essay now on 'A Day at the Seaside'.

The whole holiday was like a dream. I forgot that I ever had a past existence on the farm, though I did send a postcard to Jessie and the herd, saying, 'The sea is awful nice.' The days were filled to overflowing. Long hours spent digging castles in the sand, splashing in and out of the sea, eating unfamiliar food in our lodgings, rowing in a small oary-boat, or taking trips across to Berwick.

Here was an even bigger town then Jedburgh, with ramparts, an open-air market, and hundreds of people milling about the streets. There was so much to see that in one week I felt I had lived a lifetime of new experiences and was a woman of the world by the time I went home. Superior even to the herd.

On the last day my mother became a witch again and had another flash. We were all sitting on the sand staring at the sea as if trying to imprint it for ever on our memories. I had gathered a motley collection of 'things' to take home with me: shells, pebbles, slippery seaweed, and a defunct jelly-fish which was already beginning to smell.

'I have a feeling,' began my mother, but she was not sure what kind of feeling it was, except that she thought we were going to meet someone we knew. Here! as far away from home as foreign parts.

I wandered off to have a last paddle in the sea, then suddenly stood stock-still with surprise when I saw a familiar figure wading in the water with his trouser-legs rolled up to his knees. Auld Baldy-Heid!

'It's him!' I cried, running back to tell my parents, scattering shells and seaweed in all directions.

They called out to him, pleased to see a familiar face, and he came over to join us. But it spoiled my last day. I kept well in the background just in case he had his tawse in his pocket. Though he was in a jokey mood, I could not feel at ease in his presence. Surely there were plenty of other seasides where he could have gone for his holiday.

Then suddenly we were back home. I felt older and wiser having travelled so far and seen so much. What a lot I had to tell Jessie. I had brought a minding for her and for the herd. A stick of rock for Jock and a packet of tortoiseshell hairpins for Jessie.

'Ye've got mair siller than sense,' she sniffed; but she stuck one of the hairpins in her bun and seemed quite pleased with the result. As for Jock, he took a bite of rock and grunted, 'Man-lassie, I've fairly missed ye.'

Then, like everything else, the holiday faded away into the past. One could not look backwards for ever. The present moment was the only thing that mattered.

And the future?

I had a feeling things were going to happen. My father was behaving in a mysterious manner as if he had something up his sleeve.

My father would try anything once.

He liked gadgets and gimmicks, and would have been the first man on the Moon if he had known how to get there. He had the first wireless-set in the district. Now he had the first motor-car. A Tin Lizzie.

> Rattle his bones over the stones,
> He's only a pauper whom nobody owns.

The rough farm-road was pitted with holes, bumps, and ridges, unsuited for motor-vechicles. Flora and Ginger were accustomed to picking their way round the pitfalls, but the motor went barging on like a bucking broncho till it invariably stuck at the steepest turn and began to run backward. My father shouted 'Whoa!' as if he was still driving the pony and started shoogling about in his seat and tugging frantically at the brake. Seldom if ever did we have a straightforward run; but getting the motor was a wonderful adventure which opened wide windows on our restricted world.

Getting the wireless had been amazing enough. It was a monstrous machine almost the size of a wardrobe, full of wires and batteries (so why was it called wireless?) and far more temperamental than the old gramophone. When it worked at all we could hear mysterious crackles and the Savoy Orpheans pounding away in the background. The aerial, which was suspended on a high tree, frequently blew down and lay in a tangle on the ground; but now and again we could hear voices greeting us from as far away as London. It was miracu-

lous. Jessie walked past the machine at a safe distance, fearing
it might blow up at any moment, and indeed it sometimes
began to smoke as if about to explode.

The men were invited in on special occasions, to hear the
King speaking or to 'listen' to the two minutes' silence at the
Cenotaph, but they did not really believe in it. 'Thon's no'
natural,' said the herd and went stumping away, shaking his
head,

Little did I think the day would come when I would be
speaking on the monstrous machine myself. It was amazing
enough to hear a voice over the crackles saying, 'This is London
calling.'

The motor was a hundred times more temperamental.
Fashious, Jessie called it. It had to be cranked up with a starting-
handle before it showed any signs of life. Then suddenly it
would begin to shiver and shake as if struck by the ague. It
coughed and spluttered, sparks began to fly, and my father
leapt into the driving-seat and fiddled with the gears. There
was no driving test. He just took the motor into a field and
went round and round until he got the hang of it. But he never
quite mastered its mysteries, and even in later years when he
bought bigger and better cars he was more at home with horse-
flesh than with horse-power.

Though it widened our horizons in so many ways it was a
long time before we lost our fear of the motor.

'Pomp the horn!' my mother would cry when we emerged
into the main road or came near a corner. Even though we
were travelling at a snail's pace there was always a sense of
danger. Father knew nothing of the inner workings of the
engine, and when we stuck, he used to get out, open the bonnet
and fiddle away at the 'internals', with a perplexed expression
on his face.

We never went on an expedition without having some mis-
hap. We ran short of petrol, water, oil; we had frequent
punctures; the horn would start blowing and refuse to stop; we

would land in the ditch or get stuck in a snowdrift. I can remember sitting wearily by the wayside with bolts and nuts scattered around me, handing a spanner to my father while he tried to change a wheel. Often and often we had to push Lizzie home. How thankful I was when Father brought out the gig instead. At least with Flora we always got there and back again.

If we ventured off the beaten track we were sure to get lost, for my father had no sense of direction. If there was a wrong turning he took it. Often we ended in a farmsteading stuck in the mud at such an awkward angle that we could not reverse out of it. Once we almost landed in a duck-pond and had to leave the car and trudge home. My mother maintained that she never knew what walking was till we got the motor.

Yet on the occasions when Lizzie was running smoothly we found that the world had grown bigger and that we could reach places that had only been names before. Kelso! Galashiels! Kirk Yetholm where the gypsies lived! Otterburn over the Border!

But it was not only the world that was growing bigger. I, too, was shooting up.

It was a slow and painful process. Compared with animals, humans took a long time to mature. After many months the new baby in our house could not even toddle, yet I had watched a calf struggle to his feet seconds after he was born. Lambs began to run races when they were a few days old, and chickens fended for themselves as soon as they were out of the shell. We were the only ones who were backward.

It seemed to me that I had been in the world for centuries before I found myself amongst the big ones in the school, superior to the Infants, and with my hems let down; though still, alas! a peerie-top lacking in plain commonsense.

I could run faster, jump higher, reach up to top shelves, and do more things for myself without asking for help. My elders noticed it. 'Isn't she getting big?' they said, and kept asking me, 'What are you going to be?' as if I could suddenly turn into a caterpillar or a turnip.

The only thing I wanted to be was independent so that I need not beg pennies from my father but earn them for myself. In what way? I could single turnips like the Paddies, become a bondager, maybe, or a kitchie-las I could play the piano in a thumpy sort of way and turn the heel of sock with my eyes shut, but where would that get me? I had no other accomplishments except a facility for writing down the rubbish that was in my head. But would anyone ever want to buy it?

One of the texts on the wall-callendar – *A Thought for Every Day* – said: 'If at first you don't succeed, try, try and try again.' So I set to and filled all the odd spaces in an old jotter with stories about beasts, bogles, bubblyjocks, black lambs, cows with crumpled horns and pigs with curly tails. If I put people in the stories, a hero and a heroine, they were always Jock and Jessie in different guises.

So now when anyone asked me what I was going to be I knew the answer. 'A writer!'

'What?' they said in amazement. 'You've got a lot to learn first.'

Oh yes! and I am still learning.

I went and asked Jessie what she would like to be if she could choose. She was kirning at the time, turning the handle of the churn slowly and rhythmically, listening now and again to hear if the butter had come. Then I would get a drink of frothy soor-dook with its sharp refreshing tang.

'Me?' she said, giving me one of her straight looks. 'Just masel'.'

'But, Jessie, would you not like to be somebody different? The queen maybe or – let's think – a fairy godmother?'

'Dinna be daft!'

Jessie put her ear to the churn and then went on turning the handle; but suddenly she surprised my by saying in a confidential voice, 'I tell ye what I've aye wanted.'

'Go on, Jessie, tell me!'

Imagine her having secret longings! I vowed I would make them come true, whatever they were. 'What is it?'

'A nice nose.'

I looked at Jessie's hooked nose and said, 'But I like it the way it is.'

'Huh! it's no' on your face,' said Jessie grimly, and withdrew into her shell once more. A dull thud-thud from inside the churn warned her that the butter had come and she had no more time to indulge in silly flights of fancy.

I was disappointed that I could not grant her wish, but at least her confession revealed something I had never suspected. Even Jessie had a pride in her appearance, and it was high time I followed her example. I did not care a button what I looked like, up till now, and only hoped nobody was noticing me. Otherwise they would be sure to remark on my wrinkled stockings, tousled hair, lost ribbons or torn jersey. Clothes were nothing but a nuisance, and I envied the beasts who never bothered about them.

But all of a sudden they assumed a greater importance and I was forced, whether I liked it or not, to take stock of myself. I was to make a new beginning and must be kitted out from stem to stern. From Liberty bodice outwards. All because I had passed the Qualifying.

I have no recollection of sitting the exam itself. I only remember the moment when Auld Baldy-Heid came across to my desk and patted me on the head. At first I thought he was going to hit me and prepared to dodge the blow, but instead he said, 'Good for you! You've passed!'

I felt my face flush scarlet, more from embarrassment than pride. But it was not long before the master brought me down to earth. 'Mind! you'll need to watch your p's and q's at the Grammar School. You'll be up against some stiff competition there, so you'll have to pull yourself together.'

Pulling myself together meant restrictions of all kinds. Not just Liberty bodices. There would be new rules and new laws in the big school, new teachers, new lesson-books, new subjects. Latin, for example. What on earth would I make of that? I could not even speak English properly. The town teachers, I was warned, would be bamboozled if I came away with some of Jessie's or the herd's expressions. I must learn to get rid of my country accent, and stop running wild.

The nearer I came to leaving the familiar little village school the fonder I became of it and the more reluctant to say good-bye even to Auld Baldy-Heid. On the last day I felt a sudden surge of warmth towards him and wished I could put it into words. But what could I say? 'Dear Master, I love you.' He would have dropped dead and so would I.

At the end he shook hands with me. His grip was so tight that I would have winced if I had not lost all power of feeling. He might have squashed my bones to pulp without my notic-ing. All I could manage to say was 'ta-ta' which surely was the height of inadequacy.

I had to say ta-ta, too, to my school-friends. Kate from over the Border was to go to Newcastle for her Higher Education and would disappear from my ken, though we wrote stilted letters to each other from time to time. 'How are you getting on? I am getting on fine.'

I walked down the road with Bob (the braggart) who showed no signs of sorrow at my departure. 'Stuck-up thing!' he shouted and tried to trip me into the ditch. 'Away you go to your grand school.'

So I went on alone.

It was strange to be passing Auld Chuckie-Stanes for the last time. Never again would I stop and say my poetry to him. No more shivering with dread in the Dark Woods, or riding in Wat-the-Baker's cart. I would have to purchase my pencils and jotters in a strange shop in town instead of in Bella Confectionery's.

Everything was changing. But Jessie was still the same. She had the right answer for everything.

'How'll I get on?' I asked her, bewildered at the thought of the unknown future.

'Fine!' she said. 'The back's aye made for the burden.'